Marmite /mahr-mahyt/ *n. Brit, propr.*
1 a a preparation made from yeast extract and vegetable extract, used as flavouring in sandwiches and on toast. [F, = cooking-pot] **b** the most divisive foodstuff known to man.
2 *v.* to split people; to create opinions of extreme contrasting polarity. (*he has Marmited the jury*).
3 *predic.adj.* loved and hated simultaneously (*the Marmite effect*).

THE BUMPER BOOK OF
MARMITE

ABSOLUTE PRESS **A.**

First published in Great Britain
in 2009 by

Absolute Press
Scarborough House
29 James Street West
Bath BA1 2BT
Phone 44 (0) 1225 316013
Fax 44 (0) 1225 445836
E-mail info@absolutepress.co.uk
Website www.absolutepress.co.uk

© Absolute Press

Publisher
Jon Croft
Creative Director
Matt Inwood
Design
Matt Inwood and Claire Siggery
Editing
Andrea O'Connor

A catalogue record of this book is available
from the British Library

ISBN 13: **9781906650124**

Printed and bound in the UK
by Butler, Tanner and Dennis

An honourable mention

No yeasts were harmed in the making of
this book. All of the yeast puns and
Marmite-related ideas used herein led long,
happy lives, free-roaming and fermenting in
the minds of a band of creatives and
hatched onto page with the utmost of care.

That band of creatives had a leader of sorts:
Matt Inwood – a man with a big Marmitey
stick (akin to a Twiglet, probably) who
prodded and pointed the way. It requires a
man with a stick not least so that due
acknowledgement might be paid to all who
partook in this ridiculously wonderful book.
The following is ordered in a roughly
chronological fashion. It starts with the
parents and guardians of Marmite –
Unilever – to whom so many thanks are due,
not only because they allowed so much fun
to be had with their 107-year-old baby, but
also because their enthusiasm and support
were responsible for liberating every mind
that came to work on the book thereafter.
Special thanks, therefore, to Matt Burgess,
David Titman and Noam Buchalter at Unilever.
Jon Croft publishes many glorious books
and sets out to do so each time for that most
admirable of reasons: because he has an
unwavering passion for it. He blessed and
backed this idea from Day 1. Commissioning
Editor Meg Avent gave it her blessing from
Day 2. This book threatened to be more
sow's ear than silk purse before Claire
Siggery allied her design skills with those of
the man who carried the big Marmitey stick.
She gave up many hours and a session of
spa treatments to help see it completed, and
without her it would not be the thing of
yeasty beauty that it is. Andrea O'Connor
did not once soapbox her preference for her
native Vegemite; instead she took care of
countless editorial and administrative needs
and laughed in the majority of right places.

Then there are many who contributed with
ideas and words and pictures and little short
of all-round genius. They are most notably:

Andy Langley, who put words onto page
with such reassuring refinement and who
helped considerably and considerately
when it came to formulating a flat plan (or a
book map, as he so hates to have it called).
There was also John (Henry) Dixon who hit
a wall only to decide to leap it at the
eleventh hour and weigh in with a few
thousand words, several hundred of which
did not require censoring. And the very

gifted food writer Signe Skaimsgard Johansen,
who invented three courses of blindingly
good food for a gourmet menu. Jay Taylor
donated 26 jewels to this book and is most
probably still trying to clear a yeasty smell
from his studio to this day. His wit and skill
transformed a very simple idea into the visual
scaffold for the book. Ed Clews is another
who's inimitable works of comic genius
helped to form a dazzling alternative history.
Kate Forrester lovingly created three very
elegant typographical pieces. Andy Pedler
brought the office to a dropped-jaw
standstill when each of his highly stylised
beautiful pieces lit up on screen for the first
time: a good friend and a true artist.
Steven Roberts also chimed in with a trio of
pictures that were brilliantly clever and
witty. David Humphries delivered the most
simple but head-noddingly good and cute
images in the book. Derek Stanley was the
first person commissioned for the book and
his graphic novella did not disappoint. And
Rohan Daniel Eason's dark and magical
'Discovery' picture illustrates the most
charming scene in these 144 pages.

Wonderful ideas also came flooding in from
the following army of Marmite soldiers:
Richard Sparks (at the death – thank you!),
Ed Grace (so many wonderful little people!),
Gemma Robinson (birds and bikini bottoms!)
Ben Clay (superhero!), Richie Evans
(marvellously monstrous!), Lynn Hatzius
(such a beautiful factory!), Maria Bowers
(last-minute design help, thank you!),
Harriet Cooper (lost in battle, sorry!),
Rachel Williams (sweet sketches!) and
Rebecca Cooke (perfectly painted dregs!).

And a final mention should go to the person
who did more to enable this book than most,
whose support was sought and needed often:
Charlotte. She put up with the man and his
big Marmitey stick when he left for that dark,
yeasty world on many an evening and
weekend. Sorry. And thank you so much.

Getting us off the hook

It should go without saying that much of
what features in this book has been
delightfully dreamed up, exaggerated or
contorted severely from the truth. Needless
to say, neither the publishers nor Unilever
Plc encourage the painting of dogs, the
baiting of dinosaurs nor pillow-fighting with
a half-dozen weight of Marmite jars snuck
inside your case. We encourage you only to
eat, drink and occasionally sniff.

Roll call

These lot gave their all in battle and deserve to be remembered, contacted and commissioned again. We salute you!

Maria Bowers
www.bluesunflower-creative.co.uk
Ben Clay
clayhead84@hotmail.co.uk
Ed Clews
www.edclews.com
Rebecca Cooke
bexx19@hotmail.com
Harriet Cooper
shrooms44@hotmail.com
Kate Forrester
www.kateforrester.com
Ed Grace
www.edgrace.co.uk
Lynn Hatzius
www.lynnhatzius.com
Rohan Daniel Eason
www.rohaneason.com
Richie Evans
http:/digitalrich.deviantart.com
David Humphries
www.davidhumphries.com/
Andy Pedler
andy.pedler@virgin.net
Steven Roberts
www.sevenrobotsdesign.com
Gemma Robinson
www.gemma-robinson.co.uk
Richard Sparks
www.epoque.co.uk
Derek Stanley
www.derek@ergohub.co.uk
Jay Taylor
www.scribblejay.co.uk
Rachel Williams
www.missrachelle.co.uk

Some copyrighted materials

Original *King Kong* photograph, page 116
© United Archives GmbH/Alamy

Original *Psycho* photographs, page 115,
Top-left, Top-right and below-left
© Photos 12 / Alamy Right
Below-right © Pictoial Press Ltd / Alamy

Original *Last Supper* photograph,
pages 104–105 © ArkReligion.com / Alamy

Original *Mona Lisa* photograph,
page106 © The Art Archive / Musée du
Louvre Paris / Alfedo Dahli Orti

And one further bit of dull stuff, then promise that's it...

Marmite® is a registered trademark.
All Marmite copyright material and registered trademarks are reproduced with the kind permission of the Unilever Group of Companies.

And to anyone we managed to miss, mistake or misquote... our sincere apologies.

THE GREAT BIG MAP OF THE BUMPER BOOK OF MARMITE

Welcome... (art and words: Marmitey Stick Man) / **Chapter 1: A long time ago in a factory far, far away** (art: Marmitey Stick Man) / *The Discovery* (art: Rohan Daniel Eason / words: Andrew Langley) / *Do Androids Dream of Electric Yeast?* (art: David Humphries) / *The Marmite A-Z (A)* (art: Jay Taylor / words: Andrew Langley) / *Ransom Note* (words: Marmitey Stick Man / art: Andy Pedler) / *The Marmite A-Z (B)* (art: Jay Taylor / words: Andrew Langley) / *The Birth of Marmite* (art: Benjamin Clay / words: Marmitey Stick Man) / *Meet the Mob [1 of 3]* (art: Jay Taylor and Claire Siggery / words: John Dixon) / *A Factory Visit...* (art: Lynn Hatzius / words: Andrew Langley) / *'Ere, We Want A Word With You!* (art: Richie Evans / words: John Henry Dixon) / *The Marmite A-Z (C)* (art: Jay Taylor / words: Andrew Langley) / **Chapter 2: In our Homes and in our Hearts** (art: Claire Siggery) / *The Marmite A-Z (D)* (art: Jay Taylor / words: Andrew Langley) / *Dynamite* (art: David Humphries) / *Rescuing the Dregs* (art: Rebecca Cooke / words: Andrew Langley) / *10 Alternitive Uses for the Jar* (art: Gemma Robinson / words: John Henry Dixon with Marmitey Stick Man) / *The Marmite A-Z (E)* (art: Jay Taylor / words: Andrew Langley) / *10 Ways to Use and Abuse* (art: Gemma Robinson / words: John Henry Dixon) / *This is the Food of Nightmares* (art and words: Kate Forrester) / *Super Marmite!* (art: Ben Clay / words: Marmitey Stick Man) / *The Marmite A-Z (F)* (art: Jay Taylor / words: Andrew Langley) / *The Marmite A-Z (G)* (art: Jay Taylor / words: Andrew Langley) / **Chapter 3: Kitchen Alchemy** (art: Andy Pedler) / *A 3-Course Marmite Menu* (art: Marmitey Stick Man with Claire Siggery / words: Signe Skaimsgard Johansen) *Meet the Mob [2 of 3]* (art: Jay Taylor and Claire Siggery / words: Andrew Langley) / *The Marmite A-Z (H)* (art: Jay Taylor / words: Andrew Langley) / *The Marmite A-Z (I)* (art: Jay Taylor / words: Andrew Langley) / *John Henry Dixon's Marmite-Crusted World* (art: Richard Sparks / words: John Henry Dixon) / **Chapter 4: Between Love and Hate** (art: Andy Pedler) / *Marmite Lovers and*

Haters (art: Ed Grace) / *The Marmite A-Z (J)* (art: Jay Taylor / words: Andrew Langley) / *10 Ways to Say I Love Marmite* (words: Marmitey Stick Man) / *A Dark Evil* (art and words: Derek Stanley) / *10 Ways to Say I Hate Marmite* (words: Marmitey Stick Man) / *The Marmite A-Z (K)* (art: Jay Taylor / words: Andrew Langley) / *Marmite Heaven* (art: Steven Roberts) / *Poetry Corner* (art: Rachel Williams / words: Maritey Stick Man) / *Marmite Hell* (art: Steven Roberts) / *The Marmite A-Z (L)* (art: Jay Taylor / words: Andrew Langley) / *Creepy Marmite* (art: David Humphries) / *Hate Beyond the Clouds* (art and words: Marmitey Stick Man with John Henry Dixon) / *Meet the Mob [3 of 3]* (art: Jay Taylor and Claire Siggery / words: John Henry Dixon) / *Romeo and Juliet* (art: Rohan Daniel Eason) / *A love Like Ours Lasts Forever* (art: Kate Forrester) / *Letters of Complaint* (art: Marmitey Stick Man / words: John Henry Dixon) / *His Yeasty Breath* (art: Richard Sparks / words: Marmity Stick Man) / *The Marmite A-Z (M)* (art: Jay Taylor / words: Andrew Langley) / *10 Gestures of Love* (words: John Henry Dixon) / *Eau De Mar'mite* (art: Marmitey Stick Man) / *I'd Love to Swim...* (art: Kate Forrester) / **Chapter 5: Adventures Through History** (art: Ed Clews, with page design by Claire Siggery / words: Andrew Langley) / *The Marmite A-Z (N)* (art: Jay Taylor / words: Andrew Langley) / *The Marmite A-Z (O)* (art: Jay Taylor / words: Andrew Langley) / *The Marmite A-Z (P)* (art: Jay Taylor / words: Andrew Langley) / *The Marmite A-Z (Q)* (art: Jay Taylor / words: Andrew Langley) / **Chapter 6: A Cultural Phenomenon** (art: Marmitey Stick Man) / *The Last Tea* (art: Claire Siggery / words: John Henry Dixon) / *Mona Lisa* (art: Claire Siggery / words: Marmitey Stick Man) / *The Marmite A-Z (R)* (art: Jay Taylor / words: Andrew Langley) / *Marmite Carnival* (art: Steven Roberts) / *Dark Side of the Spoon* (art: Claire Siggery) / *Never Mind the Bovril...* (art: Claire Siggery) / *Yeasts Away!* (words: John Henry Dixon) / *The Marmite A-Z (S)* (art: Jay Taylor / words: Andrew Langley) / *Complimentary Marmite-Toasted Breakfast* (design and words: Marmitey Stick Man) / *King Kong* (photo manipulation: Claire Siggery) / *The Marmite A-Z (T)* (art: Jay Taylor / words: Andrew Langley) / *The Marmite A-Z (U)* (art: Jay Taylor / words: Andrew Langley) / *Yeast Weekly* (art: Maria Bowers, Claire Siggery, Jay Taylor, Marmitey Stick Man, Brenda Brown / text: John Henry Dixon [Marmity Bowls]; Marmitey Stick Man [Ma Might]; Claire Siggery [Unleash The Yeast Goddess...]; Andrea O'Connor [Crossword]; Marmitey Stick Man and John Henry Dixon [Looking to Meet]) / **Chapter 7: A Dark and Dirty World** (art: Andy Pedler) / *The Boys... Exposed* (art: Marmitey Stick Man and Jay Taylor / text: Marmitey Stick Man / *The Marmite A-Z (V)* (art: Jay Taylor / words: Andrew Langley) / *The Marmite A-Z (U)* (art: Jay Taylor / words: Andrew Langley) / *We Can Help* (art: Claire Siggery and Andy Pedler / words: Marmitey Stick Man) / *The Marmite A-Z (X)* (art: Jay Taylor / words: Andrew Langley) / *The Marmite A-Z (Y)* (art: Jay Taylor / words: Andrew Langley) / *The Marmite A-Z (Z)* (art: Jay Taylor / words: Andrew Langley) / *Goodbyes They Never Do Come Easy...* (art and words: Marmitey Stick Man) / *Goodbye* (art: David Humphries).

Welcome...

...to a dark
and deeply
[un]pleasurable place;
a heavenly [hellish]
celebration
of all there is to
love [hate] about the
one who goes by the
name of Marmite.

Chapter 1

A long time ago in a factory far, far away....

From the Diary of Horace Beevitamin , October/November 1902

[Beevitamin was a leading foodstuffs prospector in the late 19th century.
As a young man he took part in the Alaskan Pickled Onion Rush of 1882, and later made a fortune
after striking ketchup in California. Beevitamin, a complex character, soon gambled this away,
and was reduced to dealing in second-hand pikelets from a stall in Hackney.
His chance of redemption came when he heard strange rumours about the defunct suet mines
beneath the brewing capital of Burton-on-Trent, and decided to explore them.
Something magical, he had been told, lurked there.]

The *Discovery*

Tuesday October 14th

Joost[1], Lydia[2] and I settle into our digs at the Lurcher and Gusset public house. A decent enough place on the outskirts of Burton-on-Trent, though the food is on the dreary side. Nothing to spread on our teatime toast. Very poor. Beer, on the other hand, very good.

Wednesday October 15th

Up early with slight headache. Breakfast a disappointment. Nothing savoury to poke into our boiled eggs. We gather up our tackle and set off for a first look at the mines[3]. No-one has apparently been down them for years. We have to pull away cobwebs and a few planks from the shaft entrance. The faint smell of suet hangs in the air. We secure our rope ladder, lower the kit and prepare for the big day tomorrow. Look forward to a refreshing glass of Burton ale.

Thursday October 16th

Up early with slight headache. Skip breakfast but order a packed lunch from our landlady. We arrive at the mine before sun-up and Joost lights our Davy lamps. Then we clamber down into the Stygian gloom of the mine. I release Lydia, and she rides happily on my shoulder. Tunnels in fair condition, though occasional mounds of spent saveloy casings[4] make the going slippery. After three miles underground we stop for lunch. Meat paste sandwiches abominable. Even Lydia won't touch them. Return to the pithead. An unproductive day.

[The weeks that followed brought no joy to the underground explorers. The lack, of both success and palatable food, lowered their spirits. Then at last their luck changed.]

Thursday November 20th

Eureka! The crowning day of my life. Bad start though. Drag myself out of bed at midday with a splitting headache. Wake Joost, and we each have two pints of stout for breakfast. Lydia a shandy. Descend into the old workings beneath Blenkinsop's Nut Brown Ale Brewery[5]. Unpromising at first, with large pools of suet waste to negotiate. Then the tunnel clears and seems to run straight and level for a mile. Packed lunch worse than ever. Joost, now looking very rough indeed, suggests we give up. Also states he is very thirsty. But some strange primeval force impels me onwards. Another hundred yards and Lydia suddenly swoops from my shoulder and flutters ahead with shrill cries. We hurry after her. In the distance, something glitters By the light of the lamps we see the canary[6] perched on a pile[7] of what looks like jewels. On closer inspection it turns out to be a mound of dark glass jars, bearing bright labels. I pick one up, blow away the dust, and read the word "MARMITE". Underneath I can just make out "Yeast Extract". Somehow I know this is it! Joost, looking much revived now, unscrews a jar and smears some of the contents on his packed lunch bread and butter. The look of joy on his face as he masticates confirms to me that we have found something mighty valuable.

[And so it proved. Beevitamin's name may have faded from history, but his great discovery has been doing us good ever since.]

---

[1] Joost X. Tracht, a fellow prospector of Dutch extraction.

[2] Beevitamin's free-flying canary, whose function was to indicate (by dying) the presence of poisonous gases in the tunnels.

[3] Suet had been mined in the Burton area since Tudor times. The system of tunnels expanded rapidly during the Industrial Revolution, especially after the invention of the steak and kidney pudding by Samuel Crompton. The yield of suet ore (never very profitable) fell during the early nineteenth century, and the mines were shut down in the 1850s.

[4] The saveloy was developed in the 1750s by Richard Arkwright specifically to make use of the gristly byproduct of suet refining.

[5] Blenkinsops (catchphrase: "It's Blenkin Good For You") merged with Kecks Ales (catchphrase: "Get Your Kecks Down") in 1898, but the new company closed soon after.

[6] Industrial archaeologists believe that the name and the bright yellow colouring of the Marmite "lid" was adopted in honour of Lydia.

[7] This "pile" was part of a rich seam of Marmite which had tumbled out after being exposed by a rock fall.

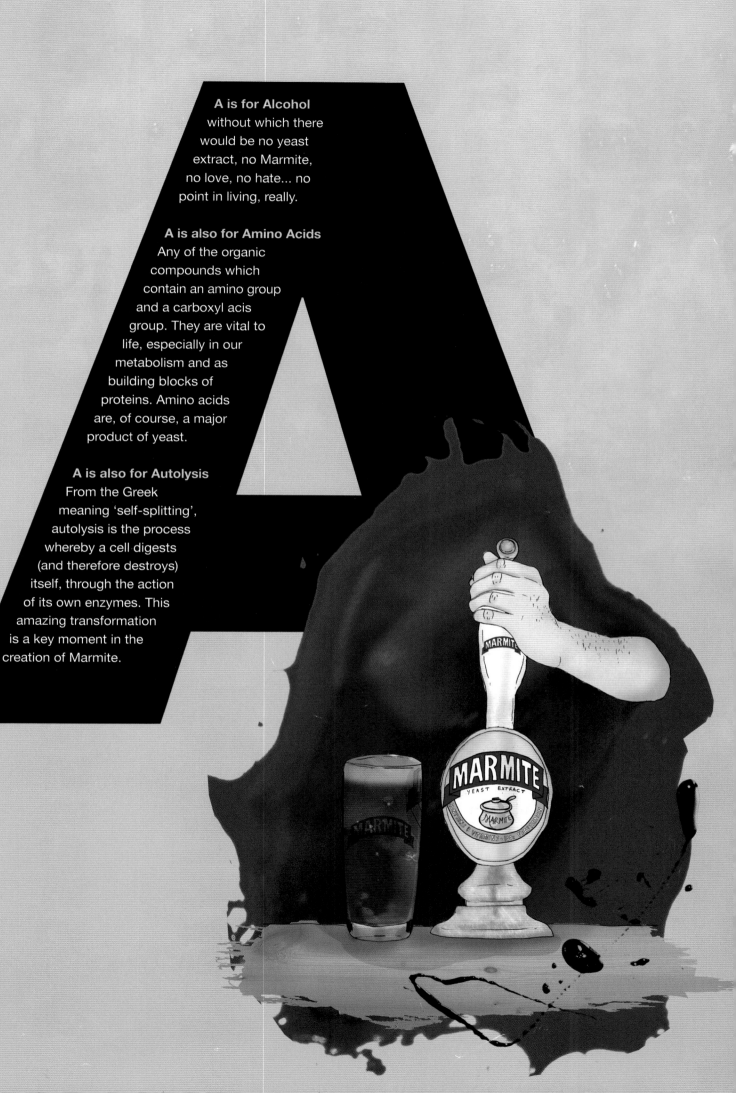

A is for Alcohol
without which there
would be no yeast
extract, no Marmite,
no love, no hate... no
point in living, really.

A is also for Amino Acids
Any of the organic
compounds which
contain an amino group
and a carboxyl acis
group. They are vital to
life, especially in our
metabolism and as
building blocks of
proteins. Amino acids
are, of course, a major
product of yeast.

A is also for Autolysis
From the Greek
meaning 'self-splitting',
autolysis is the process
whereby a cell digests
(and therefore destroys)
itself, through the action
of its own enzymes. This
amazing transformation
is a key moment in the
creation of Marmite.

If YOU EVER WANT to SMELL

YOUR beloved cLEan BREATh

Again reAd on carefully-

I WANT THE mARmiTE IN MY

possession BY 2.4 HUNDRED

HOURS ToNight- LEAVE it it in the

UNLOCKED BOOT of YOUR Car. I WANT USED JARS ONLY. DON'T try NO FUNNY STUFF either: I'll BE WITH a KNIFE AND NOT AFRAID to Spread IT AROUND.

B is for Burton-on-Trent
The great brewing town of Britain, where exceptional beers have been produced for more than a millennium. Burton is especially famed for its pale ales, whose exceptional quality is due to the local water which is rich in gypsum and other dissolved salts. It was here that Marmite began operations in 1902.

B is also for Barm
The lovely creamy foam created by yeast which rises to the top of fermenting malt.

B is also for Beri-beri
One of the many diseases brought on by Vitamin B deficiency. It is a nervous disorder which was rife amongst peoples who eat mainly milled rice. Among the other deficiency diseases are marasmus, atrophy of the lymphoid tissues, hydropericardium, scurvy and rickets. Marmite has been used in the fight against all of these ailments.

LOVE
BURTON-ON-TRENT

HATE
BURTON-ON-TRENT

The Birth of Marmite

It was French chemist and microbioligist Louis Pasteur who realised that the cells contained within yeast were in fact living plants. And it was a German scientist called Justus Liebig who then went on to make yeast into a concentrated food product. Completely overshadowing the achievements of both men, however, and probably that of every other significant 20th century event, was the creation of the Marmite Food Extract Company in 1902 by Frederick Wissler and George Huth. They opened a small factory in Burton-on-Trent, took a couple of years to get the recipe just right and then kicked back and watched the world gasp in equal amounts of admiration and disgust. When, 67 years later, Neil Armstrong would acknowledge that he had made one small step for man and a giant leap for mankind, many recognised in his words a nod to the famed rousing speech given by Wissler at the factory's opening ceremony, when he spoke of, 'this yeast extracty stuff – happen folk will thank us for it one day... I think it could catch on'. And so it was.

MEET THE MOB...

JOE "FOLIC" MARMITI

THEO "MIN" MINNESOTA

Joe "Folic" Marmiti: known to dispose of unhelpful associates in an acid bath. Pulled the plug on the Dripping Racketeers and disposed of Sid "Bubbles" Sprout. Wants to dissolve a monastery, A psychopath.

Theo "Min" Minnesota. The Don. Suffocation is his chosen method: he spreads himself across his victims until they are toast. Has been known to unscrew his head and drown people in his neck. Deaf on one side. Mentally stable.

SID
"KNEES IN"
MARMITI

Joe's big brother, Sid "Knees in" Marmiti has a fondness for making opponents double up in agony whilst reconsidering their view. Keen on billiards. He has real balls. Psycopathic tendencies.

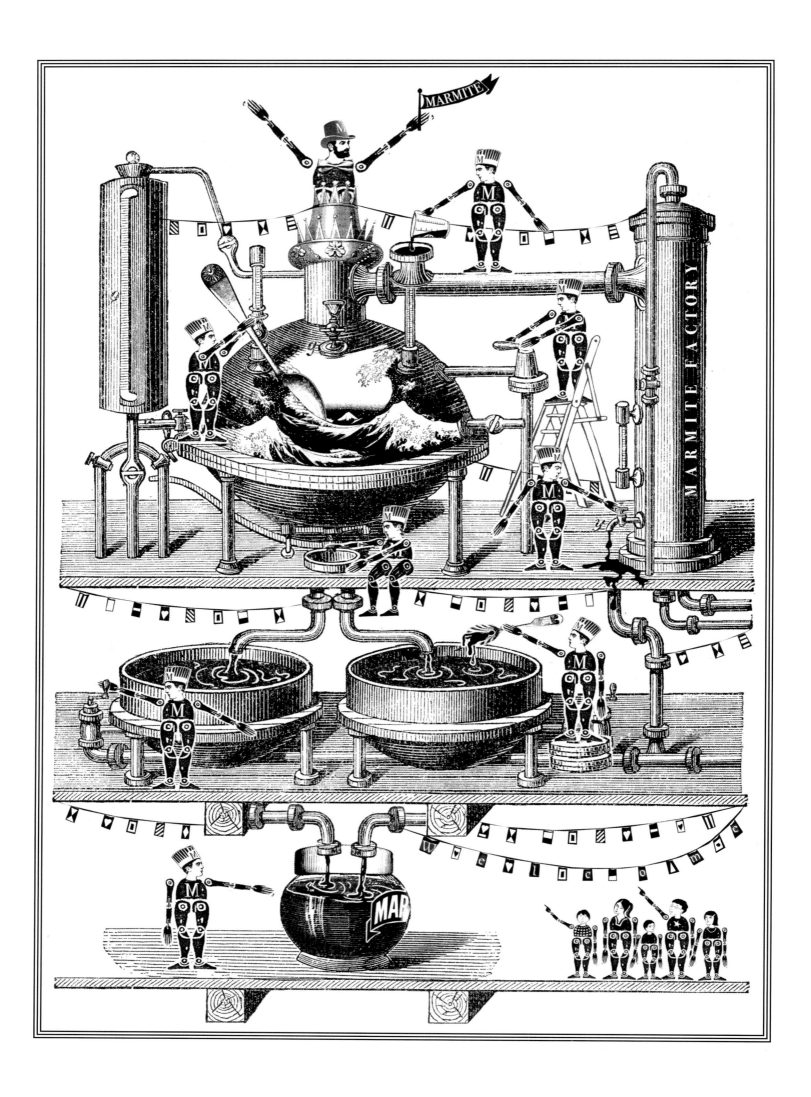

"RECLUSIVE EXTRACT BOSS FLINGS OPEN THE GATES"

writes Wallie Winker

FOR FIVE SCHOOLKIDS, IT WAS A DREAM COME TRUE.

YESTERDAY, THEY BECAME THE FIRST OUTSIDERS IN MORE THAN 100 YEARS TO SEE THE INSIDE OF BURTON'S LEGENDARY MARMITE FACTORY. GREETED AT THE GATES BY "MISTER MARMITE" HIMSELF, SIR MARMADUKE SPREADMEISTER, THEY WERE GIVEN A CONDUCTED TOUR OF THE FABLED WORKS, ENDING WITH A SLAP-UP FEAST IN THE BOARDROOM.

FEAST OF YEAST

The young visitors (all under ten) were the lucky finders of the five yellow tickets hidden in jars of Marmite which were placed at random on shop shelves up and down the land. One of the winners was Augustus Facestuffer. Augustus (9) said, "It was amazing. The bit I liked best was the Yeast Extract Room, where everything was made of Marmite. There were Marmite wine gums, a Marmite fountain, a Marmite bouncy castle and even Marmite toilet paper in the loo."

Verruca Snot (8½) , from Yeast Grinstead, was entranced by the Inventing Room. "Do you know, they're inventing Marmite butter? That way, you only have to spread it once on your toast!" Meanwhile, Mike Twittering (47) enjoyed himself in the Beer Tasting Room, watching the antics of the squirrels, whose job is to inspect the quality of new brews. "They were all completely rat-arsed," he chuckled.

NEVER A DAHL MOMENT

One of the youngsters got a lot more than he bargained for. Charlie Jamjar (9), the only winner from Burton itself, ended up by being given the entire Marmite factory, and made heir to Sir Marmaduke's considerable fortune. Most astonishing of all, he was let in on the Secret Formula - hitherto known only to the seldom-seen boss himself.

"He struck me as a nice steady lad," said a beaming Mister Marmite. "He's local - yeast in his veins. Just the sort to carry on the proud tradition". Charlie later admitted he was "over the moon".

OOMPA, LOOMPA, STICK IT UP YOUR JOOMPA

So the great day ended, and the children all agreed they would never be the same again. Augustus is now ten feet tall, Verruca is covered in garbage and Violet-Elizabeth Bott is a tasteful shade of puce. Mike is experimenting with a recipe for squirrel-flavoured Marmite. And Charlie, of course, is the new Emperor of Extract, the Sultan of Spread, the Yahweh of Yeast. Let's hope it's not another hundred years until the next great Marmite moment.

'ERE, WE WANT A WORD WITH YOU!

So you get all the feelings do you? You love it, you hate it – but what about us? Do you ever spare a thought for what we do? No, we thought not. Well it's time you horrible lot, sitting and masticating or gagging in your sad little rooms in your selfish little worlds, gave us a bit of credit. It's not you, you know, it's us. We decide how your receptor cells are tickled. If we feel like it, we might whack a bit of saltiness on your tongue or some sourness on your soft palate.

Then again we could stick bitterness on your epiglottis or sweetness on your epithelium. Sometimes we chuck some umami about and then, even if you think you hate it, you'll still want some more after half an hour. All in all we generally muck about with your transmembrane proteins and screw up your sensory neurons. And do we get any respect for it? Do we heck! So next time you spit out or gulp down some Marmite, remember: we made you do it!

C

C is for Chefs

'Yup. I'm a Marmite fan,' says Heston Blumenthal. He uses it in, among other things, his Vegetarian Pot-au-Feu at the Fat Duck. Gary Rhodes has devised a special Marmite menu – including an ice cream course. Several other high-profile chefs have expressed their enthusiasm for the stuff – though many more doubtless keep theirs hidden.

C is also for Cube

The Marmite Cube was first introduced in 1936. The 'penny' cube, as it was known, came in green boxes of six In 1995, a brand-new Marmite Cube was launched.

CHAPTER 2

In our Homes
and in our Hearts

D is for Dregs
Some classic beers are
bottle conditioned. This
means they go on maturing
in the bottle. It also mean
they throw a sediment,
which you'll see in the
bottom of the glass. This
is in fact yeast – the same
material used to make
Marmite.

D is also for Divisive
Marmite, famously, divides
the world into two groups –
those who love it and those
who hate it. So see *Love*
and *Hate*.

Rescuing

the dregs

It's a question that has engaged many a great mind...

How do I get that last bit of Marmite out of the jar?

The Marmite eater has one big problem: how to get the last little bits out of the jar. Too good to leave, but tantalizingly hard to extract. The jar's no help. Marmite sticks up in the 'shoulders' and down in the corners. There are only three solutions – and they've taken 100 years to think up.

1 Stick your finger in. Trouble is, it's on your finger. You'll have to lick it off.

2 Pour in hot water. Trouble is, it's diluted. You'll have to pour it into a mug and drink it.

3 Use a teaspoon or knife. Trouble is, it's fiddly. You'll have to be patient.

10 Uses for Your Jar

Once the contents of our beloved jar have been consumed it must stay consumed, to be processed and given back to the earth in an altogether very different vitamin-and-mineral depleted state. But our beloved brown container can be rethought, resurrected... it just takes a little imagination. See here, then, for invaluable suggestions of how to give life once more to this beautiful umber-tinged glass vessel. (Or you could just smash it into a million tiny shards of 'Marmite Past' and deposit into the depths of the 'brown' hole at your nearest glass recycling centre.)

1. as polarised lenses (simply fit into existing frames) **2.** as a jacuzzi for your gerbil (requires drinking straw to create bubbles) **3.** as a 30,000-all-seater stadium for insects (the Millipede Dome) **4.** as a goldfish bowl for tiny sun-shy swimmers **5.** as a night-light holder for dim romantics **6.** as a space helmet to transform your Action-Men into intrepid explorers of space by inverting the jar over their heads **7.** as a temptation to coax your veggie friends over to the dark side of the force (simply decant Bovril into the empty Marmite jar) **8.** as a practical joke to use on your Aussie friends (simply decant Vegemite into the jar, turn it upside down and then hide in wait). **9.** as lawn bowls (roll towards the yellow lid side) **10.** as a replacement shell for a battle-injured snail

E is for Elton
In 1979, while on tour in the former Soviet Union, Elton John got a sudden hankering for Marmite and other good old British items. An urgent request was sent to London, and a jar was swiftly smuggled into Russia in a diplomatic bag, for Elton's mouth only.

E is also for Empty
The condition of a Marmite jar when you've eaten the entire contents. Time to buy a new (full) one.

10 Ways to Use & Abuse

1. Air-raid precautions

To conceal your position from enemy aircraft at night during an air-raid, go one better than merely using black-out curtains: smear your windows with Marmite. No chink of light will now be seen and your safety is enormously improved. It will all wash off easily with warm water after the war.

2. Undetectable Forgeries

Cover a tray with about half-an-inch of Marmite. Stick lots of matchsticks into it and, Hey Presto!, you have created your very own three-dimensional Lowry painting.

3. Washing-up Liquid

Do you have plates and bowls that have deeply-ingrained marks which you can't remove? Simply use Marmite instead of washing-up liquid and you will find that the marks will never be seen again.

4. Controlling your garden

Reduce the time you spend mowing the lawn by slowing down the growth-rate of the grass. Simply shovel Marmite at strategic intervals over your lawn, then spread evenly to ensure that the whole lawn is covered. You will soon begin to notice that fewer and fewer trips to the lawn-mower shed are required.

5. That sun-kissed look

Afraid of being seen on the beach at the beginning of your holiday? Acquire your very own fake tan by rubbing handfuls of Marmite into your skin, instantly looking as though you have been tanning for weeks. Beach babes and hunks in trunks will soon be queueing up to lick you.

6. Dog Breeding

Adopt several white mongrels in need of a home. Cover their bodies with blobs of Marmite. Once dry, advertise the dogs in *Dalmatian Monthly* or some such organ and you will find that you can bash them out at around £500 a throw.

7. Tableau of tits

Erect very fine near-invisible nets around your garden to a height of about 40 feet. Sparrows, blue tits, robins and such like should soon become entangled in the mesh. Remove them, dip their feet into some Marmite and then adhere them to fences, bird-tables and other garden furniture to create a wonderful, semi-still life, squawking tableau of woodland life.

8. Marmite night lights

Buy specially wire-stiffened wicks and place into full jars of Marmite. Dot them round the room for decoration and to create interest and amazement amongst your friends. You'll find that they won't light at all, I'm afraid. But then, think of it another way: they will never need replacing.

9. Interior Design

Brighten up dull formica kitchen surfaces by dipping a rag into Marmite and dragging it across your worktops to create an interesting 'oak-grain' finish.

10. Snack Idea

Make some toast and then spread butter followed by Marmite, not too thickly, on the top. Now eat it. You may hate it.

THAT IS ABSOLUTELY DISGUSTING!!
THIS IS THE FOOD OF NIGHTMARES
Who would want to eat this stuff?!
IT SMELLS LIKE FEET!!
BLEEUGHH!
NO MORE! NO MORE! NO MORE!
yuck
TAKE IT AWAY
I feel sick

Super Marmite!

B12!
Not cool enough to have a common pseudonym, but helps maintain healthy blood and nerve cells

Yeast!
AKA Honey Magnet
Promotes wonderful breath, making you irresistible to the opposite sex (totally unsubstantiated)

Folic Acid!
AKA Vitamin B9
Helps emotional and mental wellbeing and important for growth

F is for Fashion
'Fashion Marmite' is a term recently coined to describe designer clothing which you either love or hate. See also Westwood, Vivienne.

F is also for Facebook
Marmite has the biggest Facebook following of any food brand in the world.

F is for Folic Acid
A yellowish-orange compound which is part of the Vitamin B complex, and is efficacious in treating (among other things) pernicious anaemia.

G is for Guinness
In 2007, the Guinness
Marmite jar appeared in the
shops, in a limited edition
of 300,000. It was carefully
advertised as 'alcohol-free'.

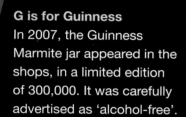

CHAPTER 3

KITCHEN
ALCHEMY

A 3-COURSE **MARMITE** MENU
BY SIGNE SKAIMSGARD JOHANSEN

IT MAY SEEM ODD TO LET A SCANDINAVIAN RUN RIOT WITH A MARMITE-INSPIRED MENU

but my British grandmother introduced the sticky brown stuff to her unsuspecting granddaughter long before I was aware of Marmite's iconic status.

MARMITE IS A FANTASTIC FLAVOUR ENHANCER and an amazing conveyer of umami. Known as the fifth taste alongside the other 'Big Four' – sweet, salt, sour and bitter – umami is integral in creating what the Japanese call 'deliciousness', a clumsy word that doesn't arouse quite so much excitement in translation.

ONE MAN WHO HAS EMBRACED THE NOTION OF UMAMI and isn't averse to using Marmite in a variety of dishes is Heston Blumenthal. I had the privilege of working as a chef stagiere in his Fat Duck Experimental Kitchen for three months and learnt more about umami from Heston and his brigade of chefs than I thought humanly possible.

THIS THREE-COURSE MENU is by no means even remotely as dazzling or sophisticated as what you'll find in Heston's Fat Duck but it does, in a small way, channel some of that enthusiasm they have for umami by deploying Marmite in each course.

It's also an extremely (and unashamedly!) indulgent roster of food, so you might wish to go easy on the portion sizes: just adjust it to your tastes.

THOSE WHO LOVE MARMITE won't need much persuading to cook with it, but sceptics too might be won over with this menu, a hybrid of a quintessentially British storecupboard icon with a sprinkling of Scandinavian flair...

Beetroot, Pancetta & Poached Egg Salad

with Marmite walnut Vinaigrette and Marmite,
Cheddar & Fennel Seed Spelt Buns

Venison Meatballs

with a Marmite, Cacao & Creme Fraiche Gravy,
Lingonberry Red Cabbage and Marmite Roasties

Marmite-Salted Butter Profiteroles

with Cardamom, Vanilla and
Popping Candy Cream filling

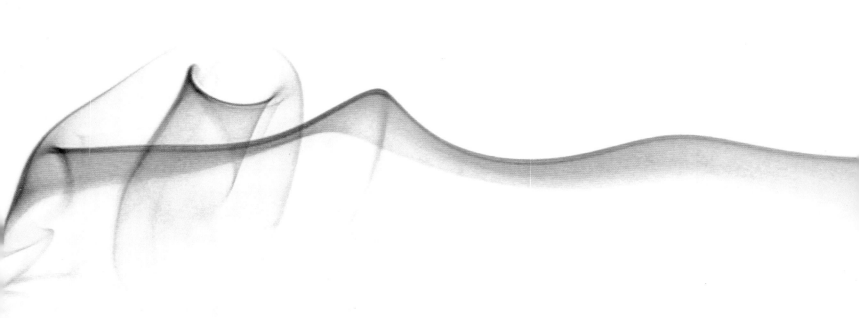

BEETROOT, PANCETTA
& POACHED EGG SALAD

WITH MARMITE WALNUT VINAIGRETTE AND MARMITE, CHEDDAR & FENNEL SEED SPELT BUNS

A riff on the archetypal 'Marmite on toast with a boiled egg'. Salad may seem boring, but if you pair it with beetroot, pancetta and a poached egg you're not going to feel too deprived. Marmite, fennel seed and cheese spelt buns are so easy to make and are moreish on their own with lashings of butter (and Marmite).

SERVES 4

For the buns (makes 12 medium buns)
15g fresh yeast
1 heaped teaspoon treacle
500g wholemeal spelt flour
1 tablespoon fennel seeds
1/4 teaspoon cayenne pepper
1/2 teaspoon dry mustard
1 tablespoon sunflower oil
300ml water
2 teaspoons Marmite dissolved in
    equal quantity of boiling water
50g grated mature Cheddar (or Red
    Leicester and gruyère)
handful of chopped and toasted
    walnuts (optional)

For the vinaigrette
1 heaping teaspoon grainy mustard
1/2 teaspoon Marmite dissolved in
    1 teaspoon boiling water
40ml cider vinegar
50ml walnut oil
black pepper

For the salad
150g pancetta (or bacon lardons)
150g cooked beetroot
mixed salad leaves (watercress,
    beetroot and spinach works well)
4 eggs

Mix the yeast and treacle in a small bowl to see if the yeast is active. It should dissolve and foam within a few minutes.

In a large bowl, sift the flour, fennel seeds, cayenne, dry mustard and make a well in the centre. Tip the yeast, oil, water and diluted Marmite into the well and beat with a wooden spoon for 5 minutes to bring the dough together.

When the dough is thoroughly mixed and looking a little bit bouncy (give it a poke) place some oiled clingfilm over the top and then refrigerate overnight.

Take the dough out when you're ready to bake the buns – it should have doubled in size – and knock back with your hands. Fold in the cheese and walnuts at this stage, kneading the dough for a 1–2 minutes until both cheese and walnuts are incorporated. Lightly oil a 12-cup muffin tray. Make little even-sized buns by rolling them between your hands – it helps if your hands are wet, that way the dough won't stick to you – place each bun in a muffin hole and then cover again with oiled clingfilm and allow to double in size in a warm place.

Preheat the oven to 220C, and place the muffin tray on the upper shelf of the oven. Bake for 5 minutes, then turn down the heat to 200C.

Make the vinaigrette by mixing mustard, diluted Marmite and vinegar in a jar or bowl. Add the walnut oil and whisk to create an emulsion. Season with black pepper to taste.

When you're ready to make the salad, simply fry the pancetta until it's crispy and evenly browned.

In a saucepan bring salted water to a simmer, then using a wooden spoon create a vortex by swirling the spoon through the water. As the water is just about to stop swirling, gently sink each whole egg in to the simmering water and cook for 2 minutes for a runny yolk, 3 minutes for a firmer one.

In the meantime, toss the salad leaves in the vinaigrette. Assemble with a scattering of beetroot and pancetta. Place each poached egg on the salad and serve with a Marmite bun on the side.

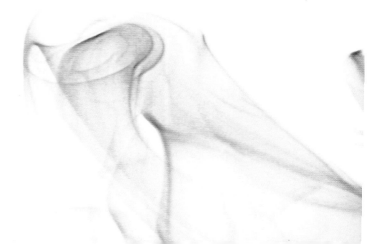

Venison Meatballs

with a Marmite, Cacao & Creme Frache Gravy, Lingonberry Red Cabbage and Marmite Roasties

Who doesn't love meatballs? This dish makes a great main course or midnight snack. Just don't do what the Swedish chef from *The Muppet Show* does and start playing tennis with the meatballs, or start waving your cooking utensils about the kitchen and shouting 'hurdy gurdy' at your mates. If you're feeding Marmite sceptics and they still prove stubborn in their resistance to Marmite's appeal then mandate a round of musical chairs. Or just ply them with plenty of wine to break their insubordination.

For the spiced lingonberry red cabbage
2 tablespoons butter
1 onion, peeled and sliced
1 apple, peeled and sliced
1/2 red cabbage, cored and sliced in thin strips
30ml cider vinegar or white wine vinegar
1 generous glass red wine
pinch of salt
2 tablespoons dark brown sugar
1 cinnamon stick
1/2 teaspoon nutmeg
5 whole cloves
5 tablespoons lingonberry jam

For the Marmite roasties
800g–1kg King Edward potatoes
4 tablespoons sunflower or grapeseed oil
1–2 teaspoon Marmite

For the meatballs
2 level teaspoons ground allspice
1 tsp ground nutmeg
1/4 level teaspoon ground ginger
1/2 onion, peeled and finely chopped
1 1/2 slices stale country bread, crusts removed, torn into small pieces (about 55g weight in total)
110ml milk mixed with a tablespoon of yoghurt
1 large egg yolk
500g venison mince
1/2 level teaspoon salt
1/4 level teaspoon ground white or black pepper

For the crème fraîche gravy
300ml beef or veal stock
4 tablespoons brandy
1 tablespoon Marmite
150ml pot full-fat crème fraîche
1 tablespoon grated cacao (don't use a sweetened chocolate)

bunch of dill for garnish (optional)

Start with the cabbage first. Melt the butter in a large saucepan, add the onion, apple, red cabbage and all the other ingredients except the sugar, spices and lingonberry jam. Cook for 1 hour, making sure to stir occasionally so the bottom doesn't burn. Add a little water if the red cabbage gets dry. When the cabbage is cooked, add the sugar, spices and lingonberry jam. Cook a further 30 minutes and taste for seasoning. A splash of red wine added to the red cabbage before serving won't go amiss

Next, prepare the potatoes. Peel and quarter the potatoes and place in a large saucepan, covering with cold water. Add some salt, cover with a lid and bring to the boil, allowing the potatoes to parboil for 10 minutes. Meanwhile, preheat the oven to 200C. Place the oil in a roasting tin and heat in the oven while the potatoes parboil. When the potatoes are almost cooked through, strain the water and place the potatoes back in the pan on the heat, give them a good shake so they dry out. They'll look a little dry and fluffy: don't worry! Add the Marmite to the hot oil, swirling around so you get an even distribution. Then add the potatoes. They should sizzle. Give them a toss with a spatula or large spoon and place in the oven, allowing to roast for 45 minutes. Next make the meatballs. Preheat

the grill to a medium-high heat. Heat 1 tablespoon of the oil in a pan and cook the onion over a low heat until soft for 8–10 minutes. As the onion goes translucent, add the spices and fry for a minute, then set aside to cool. In a small bowl, combine the bread with the yoghurt-infused milk. Make sure all the bread is moistened and leave until the liquid has been absorbed.

In a larger bowl, combine the mince, cooked onion and seasoning. Add the milk-soaked bread and egg yolk and using your hands, mix everything together. Take a spoonful of the mixture and fry off before you start rolling to check your seasoning's as it should be. Using a teaspoon's worth of meatball mixture, lightly roll between your palms to form meatballs, and either fry straight away or if you're making these in advance, set aside on a sheet covered with clingfilm and keep refrigerated until you're ready to grill the meatballs. Grill for 8–10 minutes, turning them once and grilling a further 8–10 minutes. They should be golden brown.

Now make the gravy. Bring the beef or veal stock to a boil, reduce by half and add the brandy. Allow this to cook until you can't smell any alcoholic vapours (1 minute or so), then add the Marmite, crème fraîche and grated cacao. You may need a pinch of sugar if the sauce is quite acidic from the crème fraîche, but taste to season. Add the grilled meatballs to this sauce and simmer for 20 minutes while the Marmite roasties are doing their thing.

When the red cabbage, Marmite roasties and meatballs are all cooked assemble either in a bowl or a plate. Be generous with the gravy and sprinkle with dill fronds.

MEET THE MOB..

**BIG SQUEEZE
AND
LITTLE SQUEEZE**

**BILLY
"B12"
BOMBER**

The psychopathic inseparables, Little and Big gave up an unpromising comedy career to become the most feared couple on the street. Their unfortunate victims were driven to leap from skyscraper windows rather than have to listen to their execrable routine. Falling into their hands is no joke. If there is any funny business to be done it is left to others.

Breadsticks Celeri aka Billy "B12" Bomber knows his way into a safe and woe betide anyone who gets in his way. Has always denied all charges. His catchphrase, "Blast!", was last heard on an occasion when the doors stayed on. Known to react psychopathically.

TANGYUAN "RICE CAKES" ERKUAI

NIAN GAO "JUMBO RICE CAKES"

Tangyuan "Rice Cakes" Erkuai. Formerly with the Triads, this Chinese psychopath deserted them and, via a No.34 and a No.22, arrived at the Marmiti house. He immediately set about rearranging the furniture. Only he now knows where the family gold is kept. As a result he wields enormous power and has the ear of the Don, but refuses to return it.

Now separated from his Siamese twin, at six foot ten inches Nian Gao "Jumbo Rice Cakes" Erkuai still retains his World's Tallest Child title despite the fact that he is now 47. He has been unprepared to relinquish it. Introduced to the family by his twin, he is unencumbered by intellect and has been known to chase and attack his own shadow on moonlit nights. Axes have often been found wedged in panel fences the following day. Hanged his first three hamsters. A man to agree with. Possible psychopath.

Marmite-Salted Butter Profiteroles
with Cardamom, Vanilla and
Popping Candy Cream filling

One of the many great things about Heston is his sense of fun, and popping candy – or space dust – has been featured in a number of his dessert recipes over the years. I've incorporated it into this quintessential French dessert and you should marvel at the dance going on in your mouth. Profiteroles have a timeless appeal and are a doddle to make. They can be made in advance and refreshed in the oven before you fill them with crème patisserie. The recipe for them is a standard one from the *Leiths Cookery Bible* (Bloomsbury). The inspiration for Marmite-salted butter caramel came from chocolatier Paul A. Young whose Marmite chocolate truffles and salted butter caramels always hit that umami bliss point. This is simply a spin on those two brilliant truffles. I've been parsimonious with the Marmite here, using it simply as a gentle flavour enhancer, but if you're a real keen bean for Marmite then crank it up to a full teaspoon or more...

MAKES 16 SMALL OR 12 LARGE PROFITEROLES IF YOU WANT TO SERVE YOUR MATES PROFITEROLE BOMBES

Choux pastry for profiteroles
55g butter
150g water
70g plain flour, sifted 3 times, with
  ½ teaspoon salt
2 eggs, beaten

For the popping candy crème patisserie
300ml whole milk
2 egg yolks
50g caster sugar
pinch salt
30g cornflour
½ teaspoon vanilla extract
½ teaspoon ground cardamom
  (or cinnamon or nutmeg)
50g popping candy

Marmite-salted butter caramel
300g white granulated sugar
  (unrefined sugar will increase the
  risk of crystallisation)
100g salted butter
½ teaspoon Marmite
300g double cream
½ teaspoon vanilla extract
you may need an extra pinch of salt, if
  so use something like Maldon, Halen
  Mon or grey salt but avoid table salt
  as it gives quite a harsh flavour

First, make the pastry for the profiteroles. Preheat the oven to 200C. Place the butter and water in a small saucepan and allow the butter to melt over a medium heat. When melted, turn the heat up so the liquid starts to boil and remove from the heat and immediately add the flour and beat vigorously with a wooden spoon for 20 seconds. The mixture should come off the sides of the pan. This is your *panade* which you spread on a large plate to cool down. When it is lukewarm to the touch, add the beaten egg in increments, stirring vigorously after each addition. Do this until you have a dropping consistency, or the mixture takes about 10 seconds to drop from the spoon when you raise it.

Shape the mixture into balls on a baking sheet, and pat down any spiky tops with a wet finger. Bake on the upper oven shelf for 25–30 minutes. Resist the temptation to check them halfway through cooking or they might collapse. The profiteroles should puff up and look golden brown. Remove from the oven and using the end of a small, thin spoon poke a hole in each profiterole. Remove any uncooked mixture from the inside and place upside down back on the baking tray. Bake a further 10 minutes to dry out and then allow to cool on a wire rack.

Next make the crème patisserie. Scald the milk in a saucepan. In a medium bowl whisk the egg yolks, sugar and salt until light and fluffy. Add the cornflour, stir through and then the hot milk. Stir again and pour the mixture back in the saucepan. Slowly bring to the boil whilst stirring continually. When the mixture starts to boil it will look lumpy: don't worry – this is normal. Keep stirring and it will become smooth and once this happens remove from the heat, add the vanilla and cardamom (if using) and allow to cool in a bowl. Clingfilm the surface of the crème patisserie, to prevent a skin forming, and refrigerate.

When you're ready to use the crème patisserie, place it in a bowl and whisk to make smooth again. Add some lightly whipped cream and fold through until evenly blended. Have a piping bag handy for stuffing the profiteroles.

Now make the caramel. Make sure you have a large saucepan to hand (larger than you think you might need as this foams up quite a bit). Then make sure this pan is scrupulously clean. Any impurities will increase the risk of crystalisation. If you're very concerned about crystallising the caramel, add 50ml of liquid glucose to the mixture

Have all your ingredients weighed out and to hand, together with an oven glove for holding the pan, and some iced water nearby in case you burn yourself (caramel gets extremely hot).

When you're ready to start, pour the granulated sugar into the saucepan. Allow it to melt on a low-medium heat. Be patient as the more chance you give the sugar to melt properly the less likely it will crystallise. Keep an eye on it and carefully fold over any melted sugar from the sides into the middle,

circulating the uncooked sugar so it melts evenly. Don't stir too much. If you have a sugar thermometer take the caramel to 140C. It should look like a deep copper, but not dark brown. The caramel will smoke – immediately add the butter, stir quickly, remove from the heat and then add the Marmite and double cream. Stir as vigorously as you can to enable the cream to distribute and to avoid the risk of big lumps in your caramel. If you do get lumps all is not lost, simply sift the caramel through a metal sieve when it's cooled slightly (the caramel lumps can be kept for other purposes).

Taste the caramel when it's cool, add as much salt as you think is necessary – you want a balance between the sweetness of the caramel and a good salty taste.

Fill the profiteroles with the popping candy crème patisserie, and serve in martini glasses or small bowls. Pour the caramel sauce over the top. If you like your sauce very hot, it will be less viscous so be prepared for the sauce to run. A lukewarm caramel sauce will be perfect for dunking the profiteroles in, if that's what you prefer.

Serve with cape gooseberries or a string of redcurrants for garnish.

H is for Hate
Marmite arouses very strong emotions, both for and against. Those against can visit their very own website: www.marmite.com/hate

H is also for Huth, George
One of the founders (with Frederick Wissler) of the Marmite Food Extract Company in 1902.

MARMITE

I is for Ice-cream
Chef Gary Rhodes has dreamed up a host of yeast-extract recipes, including Coffee Ice Cream with Chocolate Marmite Sauce and Marmite Syrup Coffee Ice Cream.

JOHN HENRY DIXON'S MARMITE-CRUSTED WORLD

Marmite! The very word evokes a host of memories. One's very childhood was almost defined by it. Who can forget where they were and what they were doing when that distinctive dark viscosity was first encountered? For me it is a schoolboy memory: I had just finished a rousing game of Battledore and Shuttlecock and had repaired to the Sanatorium to wax Matron's pelmets, an imposition that I had earned for some trifling misdemeanour which I cannot now recall. From my position between her casements I could see into the kitchen and there, on the table was toast, butter and a Marmite jar with the lid removed. Immediately the aroma was upon me and I knew that nobody could offer me a better spread than Matron's. From that moment on it became a great comfort to me in my somewhat yeasty youth: sandwiches on the train during my sole trip to Dover, joyful japes with my father and his friends on the annual Marmite Nouveau race from Burton-on-Trent (twice were we the first home with it), fruitless attempts to send messages in a jar when the missive was rendered illegible, a sharp and soggy pocket in my tweeds when I ended up in a tree near the bottom of the Cresta Run and we even used it to hold the bails in place during a house cricket match which was in danger of being disrupted by the Great Storm of 1924.

But innocence passes. Some years later an old friend, who later tragically lost his voice when the inside of his throat was badly bombed during the war, rang me, "Fancy a jar, old boy?" he asked. I acquiesced to this seemingly grand idea, for a few hours in his company would be a pleasure, but disaster was lurking silently in the shadows. I, dear reader, had walked innocently into a deadly ambush. I was offered a small jar. I took a taste. I expected a soothing balm. Too late, I realised that the jar before me had transmogrified from the beatific smile of a Mother Teresa to the snarling and savage grimace of a mountain wolf. This was indeed the Devil's work. There were vitamins involved. I was once again in the power of Beelzebub. Dante's inferno could not have competed with this. A small jar became a large one. A large jar became a crate. A crate became two. Was there no end to this depravity? I felt myself falling, falling, falling....

Only now can I look back upon those dark days and smile. It was my Great-aunt Sopwith's wise words that brought me back from the brink, "Marmite may be good for the brain, but a jar should never be worn under one's hat". I think we all know what she meant.

John Henry Dixon
Written as the shadows from the Irish yews lengthen upon the lawn

MARMITE SPONGE

4 Tbsps. Soap powder (non -biological)
1 pt. Water
1 pr. Motoring goggles
1 Electric fan
2 Bath sponges
A quantity of Marmite
Soap flakes
1 Tube of toothpaste
Bath salts

Put the soap powder into a liquidiser, add a little of the water and blend slowly until you get an even paste. Next put on the goggles, remove the top of the goblet, add the remainder of the water and liquidise the mixture at top speed for several minutes until your kitchen is full of bubbles from floor to ceiling. This will ensure that the consistency is nicely light. Now place four tablespoons of these bubbles in a bowl and refrigerate. At this point you should close any connecting doors to the rest of the house but open the one that leads to the garden. Plug in and turn on the fan, setting it to full speed, and wait until all the bubbles have cleared away. Spread one of the sponges with Marmite, adding a few fresh soap flakes and the other with the froth from the bowl. Place one sponge on top of the other, filling innermost, and press down firmly. Take the tube of toothpaste and write a cheery greeting on the top of the cake. Dust the top with bath salts.

MARMITE SOLDIERS

1 Wholemeal loaf
1 Carpenter's file
1 Lee Enfield rifle
Oil
Vinegar

On New Year's Day put the loaf to one side for three months. With March past, check that it it is completely rank and file off any patches of mould, then beat it with the rifle butt - corporal punishment helps to tenderise the bread. Now cut it, first into slices and then into four or five strips per slice. Drizzle with oil and vinegar. Next have a good look around your kitchen, as time spent in reconnaissance is seldom wasted, before spreading sheets of foil on your grill pan and parading the strips of bread on it in several ranks. Check their dressing to ensure that none is out of line. Now grill them fiercely, discarding those that reveal to you any more than their Name, Rank and Serial Number (this is why French bread is never used as it has a very low pain threshold and tends to give in easily). When the soldiers are seriously browned-off all over, smear them with Marmite so as to ensure that they cannot be seen at night and serve with honour.

PLAITS DU JOUR

4 Tbsps. Marmite
1 Icing Bag
Salt and Pepper

Before anything else, lay some greaseproof paper on a baking tray. Now spoon the Marmite into the bag and squeeze out three lines of Marmite onto the greaseproof paper. They should be about half an inch apart, 9 inches long and about as thick as your little finger. Wetting your hands under the tap, plait the three strips of Marmite into a sort of rope, ensuring that all the strands are evenly spaced. Place in a hot oven for about a week and then put to one side and allow to cool for 30 seconds. Slice thinly, season to taste and serve with toast.

TROUSER RISOTTO

This is extremely good for livening up a party.

1 mole
8 oz long-grain rice
2 apples
6 flies
olive oil
salt & pepper
1 pr trousers

Skin the mole and discard the carcass. Cook rice as usual and add the flies. Place an apple in each pocket, rub the oil, Marmite and seasoning into the seat of the trousers, inside and out, put them on and run around until they are at 103.4 degrees fahrenheit. Allow to cool by sitting in the fridge for ten minutes. Iron flat, add the mole skin and serve on the rice.

THRUSH BEAKS ON TOAST

This has always been one of my favourites, especially after a hard days ratting. My original recipe used anchovy sauce, but I think I now prefer Marmite.

12 thrush beaks
1 loaf
Marmite
butter

Slice the bread and toast on one side. When done, place the bread toasted side down and spread with the butter. Sprinkle the beaks evenly over this, ensuring they are in the correct pecking order and then cover them with a liberal coating of Marmite. Toast until the beaks begin to open. Discard those that do not.

You may find pre-packed beaks in the supermarkets but, for the best flavour, scour your local pet-shops for some fresh ones going cheep.

CIGARETTE AND MARMITE SOUP

Here's a dish that could become a habit!

20 low tar cigarettes
1 small glass ash-tray
4 drops nicotine essence
2 tsps. Marmite
1 pt double cream
vegetable oil

Ignoring the ill-mannered warnings on the packet, remove the filters from the cigarettes with pile-tweezers and put them aside for later. Peel the cigarettes and place the tobacco in a food processor. If you are watching your weight you may find it useful here to add a disposable lighter. Smash the ash-tray under a tea-towel with a sledgehammer or the head of a cat and put the pieces into the mixer. Blend until you have a crunchy and sparkly paste. Now slowly add the Marmite and the cream until the mixture has the texture of a small hedgehog. Add the nicotine essence, pour into a bowl and put into the fridge for half an hour. Meanwhile, in a heavy-bottomed pan, heat the oil until very hot and then flash fry the filters until they are crisp but not burnt. Scatter them over the soup just before serving. It is healthier to leave about half an inch of soup in the bottom of the bowl.

CURED HADDOCK

There is nothing more reviving than a cup of hot Marmite.

1 feverish haddock
24 Paracetamol tablets
4 blankets
Marmite

Put the haddock to bed immediately, covering it with the blankets and putting up with no nonsense whatsoever. Administer plenty of water and two Paracetomol every four hours whilst allowing no visitors. Allow nothing else to pass its lips except a thrice-daily cup of hot Marmite tea. After two days the fish will be at the correct temperature and you will be able to cook and eat it as normal, but remember to only allow it out if it is well wrapped up.

GREY MULLET WITH MARMITE

I once heard my gardener say "on me 'ead, Son." I have never forgotten it.

1 1970s footballer
1 large jar of Marmite
1 Cliff Richard CD
6 oz plain flour
8 oz cheese footballs
oil

Remove the head from the footballer and throw the rest onto the cruel scrap-heap of sporting history. Rub the Marmite into the hair and leave the head on a spike by a fence. Now put the CD on your player, turn the volume to zero and listen to it, through headphones, for fifteen minutes. Next drop the head into the flour, dribble the oil onto it and kick it into the dining room. Add the cheese footballs and immediately fall over and accuse one of your guests of tripping you up. Make sure he or she is sent to the scullery.

A SURFEIT OF LAMPREYS

I can always have too many Lampreys.

21 lampreys
fish oil
Marmite
salt & pepper

String and season the lampreys and fry until lightly browned in the oil. Spread them lightly with Marmite and season to taste. Eat twenty of them.

GRILLED STICK INSECT

This is exactly as first published in my first book, Peel the Otter (Absolute Press, 2004). Even after all these years I have been unable to improve upon it.

130 medium-sized stick insects
1 jar of Marmite

Remove the legs from the insects with a pair of vole-tweezers and discard. Do not waste time trying to remove the wings as they don't have any. Now dip the insects into the Marmite and place them under a hot grill for two minutes. Allow to cool and place in a jug. When seated, shake the jug and throw the contents onto the table-cloth. Allow each guest in turn to attempt to pick up one stick insect without disturbing any of the others. If successful, the guest may eat it and try again. If other stick insects are disturbed however, the guest must stop eating and the turn passes to the left. Given the fact that they are covered in a glutenous yeast extract, this should give you a good hour's rest before trudging back to the kitchen to resume your forced labour.

CHEESE & BILLIARDS

I find that the addition of Marmite to this traditional recipe makes it last longer.

2 oz Brie (this must be very runny)
2 oz Roquefort
1 oz Parmesan
1 oz Edam
4 oz Stilton
Marmite
3 oz Hundreds-and-Thousands
1 billiard-table
1 blowtorch
2 sticks of celery
2 pkts cheese & onion crisps.

Shut the stilton away in a kitchen drawer. Now inform all the other pieces of cheese what you are about to do, but keep the stilton in the dark. First, grate the Brie over a small camping stool. Slice the other cheeses into small strips, ensuring that you take the Parmesan by surprise. Introducing the Brie at the last minute (unless you are very familiar with this dish, surnames will suffice), fold the cheeses together, taking care to smooth out all the creases with the heel of your foot. Form this mixture into 2 inch balls, dust with flour and place them behind the baulk line on the billiard table (ignore the six 'spots': these are for a potted shrimp recipe). Check that there are no more than four balls in the 'D' and then toast them all to a rich brown with the blowtorch. Having allowed the cheese to cool, cover the baize with Marmite, sprinkle hundreds-and-thousands liberally over the table's cushions, take the two sticks of celery and, alternating with your companion, try to pot all the pieces of cheese. When there is no cheese left on the table, eat the crisps.

Chapter 4

Between
Love and Hate

We love it.

We hate it.

J is for Jesus
In May 2009 a family from Ystrad, Wales, claimed to have seen the likeness of Jesus Christ's face on the underside of a Marmite jar lid. Gareth Allen, 37, said: 'The kids are still eating it, but we kept the lid'. .

10 ways to say I Love Marmite

1. J'aime Marmite (the French way)
2. Ich liebe Marmite (the German way)
3. Ik hou Marmite (the Dutch way)
4. !SplattBuuuuurpMarmite! (the Double-Dutch way) 5. I think I am Marmite, therefore I love Marmite (the Cartesian way) 6. An extreme penchant for salty elixir in the first person (the Cryptic way) 7. It is not so much about whether I should love Marmite, but whether giving Marmite my support is the best thing for the people (the Politician's way) 8. One is rather partial, yes (the Royal way) 9. Love Marmite and the world will love Marmite with you (the Zen way)
10. Yeah, man, Marmite, what's not to love? (the Hippy way)

10 ways to say I Hate Marmite

1. Je déteste Marmite (the French way) 2. Ich hasse Marmite (the German way) **3. Vihaan Marmite (the Finnish way)**
4. I am so over Marmite, we're through (the Finished Way)
5. Freddie Starr ate my Marmite (the Tabloid way) 6. I didn't see the incident with the Marmite; I will wait until I see the replay (the Football Manager's Way)
7. Marmite is other people (the Existentialist's way) 8. And the first extract to be evicted from the Yeast Brother house is... Marmite (the Reality TV way) **9. I love Vegemite (the Australian way)**
10. I hate Marmite (the way of anyone who denies their true feelings about Marmite)

K is for Kiss
In 2003, the nation was stunned by the Marmite Kiss TV commercial. A lifeguard's enjoyment of his Marmite sandwich is interrupted by a drowning man. The guard rescues him and gives him the kiss of life. Overcome by the taste, the swimmer kisses him back, with passion. 71 viewers complained. Four years earlier another commercial and another kiss, this time between an amorous couple – one who loved and one who hated... not the longest of screen snogs!

K is also for Knife
Everyday table implement without which we would not be able to spread Marmite.

K is also for Kosher
The Really Jewish Guide has listed Marmite as suitable for a Kosher diet for many years, although it is yet to be certified as such in the UK.

**SOME EARLY SKETCHES
FROM THE NOTEBOOKS OF THE
ESTEEMED POET, W.B. YEAST**

ME SUPPER

Oh! yellow lid
Oh! umber pot
Inside you hid
My savoury shot

MY MARMITE

May nothing mar
My favourite jar
My Marmite

From afar
You look like tar
My Marmite

My savoury Tsar
My storecupboard star
My Marmite

A FEAST DARKLY

Extracted from yeast
The dark, dark beast
On which I will feast
Tonight

Should go well on some bread
Or some crumpets instead
And some butter should make it just right

THE THING I LIKE MOST

The thing I like most
To spread on me toast
Is Marmite and butter
So that's what I put there

Poetry Corner

L is for Love
The opposite of hate, and
the overwhelmingly large
feeling of most Marmite
eaters. They have the
choice of two websites:
www.ilovemarmite.com and
www.marmite.com/love

**L is also for Leeuwenhoek,
Antonie van (1632–1723)**
Known as the 'Father of
Microbiology', he pioneered
the use of the microscope.
It enabled him to study
yeast in fine detail and
discover that it was made
up of minute spherical and
ovoid cells.

**L is also for Liebig,
Justus von (1803–1873)**
German chemist who
discovered that yeast cells
could be concentrated and
eaten. He first had to solve
the problem of making the
yeast byproducts palatable.
By using autolysis and then
concentrating the result he
produced a vegetable
substance meaty in flavour,
appearance and smell.

Tommy "Rib" O'Flavin was on the way home from an
uneventful patrol. He'd been up for an hour or so
without alarm and now it was back to base and some
breakfast. It was grand above the clouds, the
troubles of the world seemed far away...............

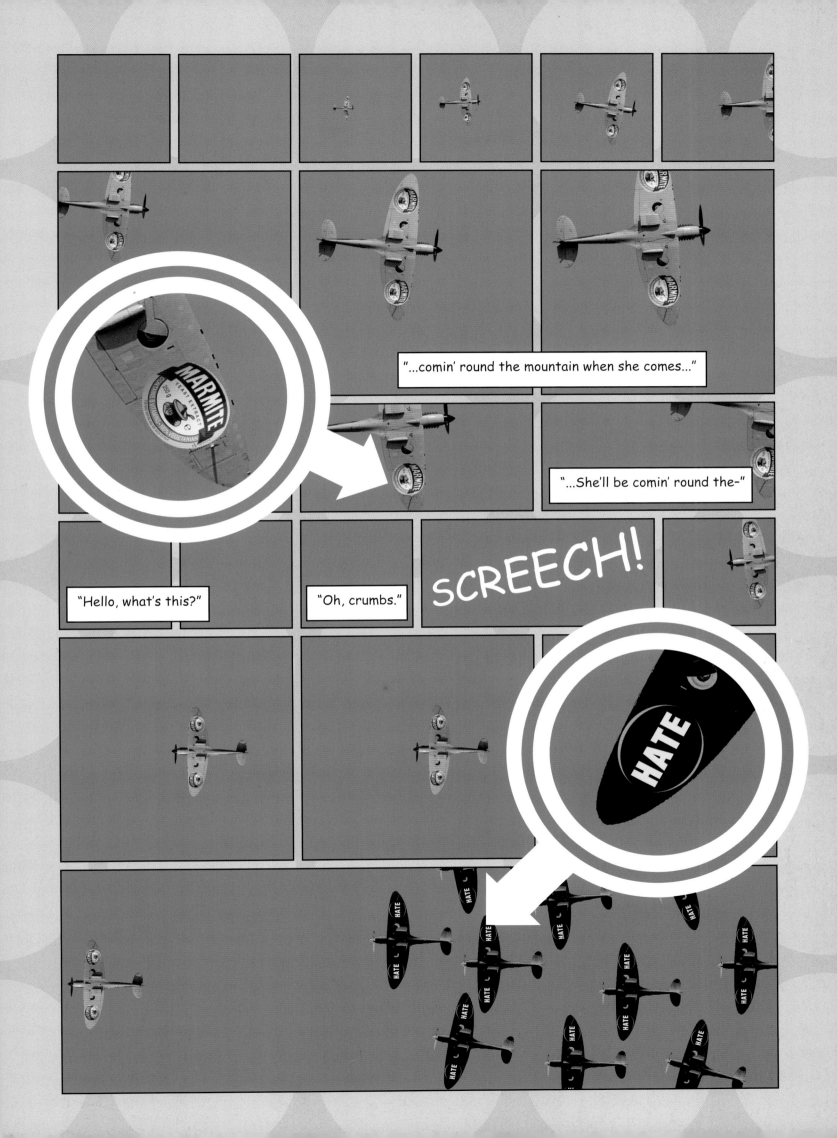

MEET THE MOB...

JIMMY "THE NUT" MARMITI

FRANKIE "FISHNETS" MARMITI

Joey "Oven-Baked" Cashews, a.k.a. Jimmy "The Nut" Marmiti always wanted to be a chef, but was forced into the family business by his father. His latent culinary talents clearly come to the fore in his cross-examination techniques: he pushes his victims into the oven and turns on the gas. Useful information has, so far, remained elusive. He sensibly has an arrangement to pay his gas bill by direct debit. There have been suggestions of psychopathy.

Frankie "Fishnets" Marmiti: So named because of his habit of covering his face with a stocking durings heists. This stood him in good stead until the general confusion during a botched attempt to hijack a trawler led to him being thrown overboard and left to float in the Atlantic undetected for more than three months. A bit of a slimy character. Psychopathy suspected.

THE CRISP BOYS

The Crisp boys have to be approached with caution. "Single" is something of a loner and values his solitude. He has been known to clear a crowded restaurant using contents of his violin case. "Six Pack" cycles everyday without seeming to get anywhere. and is seldom seen far from a mirror. Not much escapes him: he will sit up and take notice at the drop of a hat. Both of them have very brittle tempers and can snap at the slightest provocation. One of them is probably slightly more psychopathic than the other.

Romeo & Juliet

Act V
Scene III

M is for My Mate Marmite
A famous army-based TV commercial from the 1980s in which squaddies chanted 'My Mate! Who's Mate? My Mate – Marmite!'.

M is also for Marston's Marmite
A limited edition jar, made with Marston's Pedigree (one of the greatest – and yeastiest – of English beers). It was released to coincide with the 2009 Ashes Cricket series in the UK.

M is also for Meat
Nothing to do with Marmite. The uninitiated sometimes think Marmite is a meat spread, though of course it is completely vegetarian.

10 Gestures of Love

1. One evening, try to get home before your partner. Nip upstairs and cover the bottom sheet of your bed with Marmite. Finish it off by sprinkling a few rose petals over it. When you go to bed later on, say nothing and just wait to see how long it is before anything is noticed. **2.** If you are in the cinema watching a romantic movie, secretly dip your fingers into a jar of Marmite then quietly stroke your partners hair and cheek in the dark. They will love you for it. **3.** Go to the park together and throw Marmite jars at the ducks. **4.** Write little love notes in pencil on small bits of paper and hide them in his Marmite jar. **5.** Buy her Marmite lipstick. **6.** As a Forget-me-not, put a little patch of Marmite on the back of her white bikini bottoms. **7.** Put a teaspoon of Marmite in various random pages of his diary so that he will be reminded of you. **8.** Run her a steaming hot bath and add lots of Marmite to it. **9.** Ask her if she will marry you and, if she accepts, go round all the grocery shops together and buy her the biggest jar of Marmite you can afford. **10.** Secretly hide half a dozen Marmite jars in each of your pillows and then, once you are both ready for bed, start a playful pillow fight.

Letters of Complaint

Dear Sirs,

I would like to take issue with your correspondent who claims that Marmite is an *ideal* food to serve to kids. I am a breeder of goats and truly wish that I had never seen that article. To date I have had to call out the vet on sixteen occasions since I changed the diet of my new arrivals, often at dead of night, and despite his tireless efforts no fewer than nine fatalities have resulted, which represents, nearly a quarter of my trading stock. I strongly recommend that you instigate some method of regulation amongst your staff to ensure that such dangerous advice is never again given. My solicitors are aware of your business address.

Yours,

A. Beard (Mrs,)

Dear Sirs,

May I add my fourpenny-worth to the nonsense being written about the need to throw Marmite away if it has passed its sell-by date? My grandmother managed to salvage two jars of Marmite from her cabin before leaving RMS Titanic in some haste and, by secreting them in her drawers, was able to carry them back home to England via a rope-ladder, a lifeboat, RMS Carpathia, a railway carriage and a Lanchester. One of them is still in use today with no noticeable loss of flavour or any attributable illness.

Yours sincerely,

I. Berg

Dear Sirs,

Your inhaler is useless! Far from relieving my chronic sinusitis as hoped for, your foul-smelling unguent created an almost impenetrable blockage in both my nostrils and rendered the tips of two snooker cues virtually unusable. Were it not for the quick thinking of my cousin and the close proximity of a travelling corkscrew I fear the pleasures of my rose garden may have become a thing of the past.

Never again!

S. Nott

Dear Sirs,

Please cancel my subscription to your periodical with immediate effect. When I filled out the form there had been a power cut and, by the light of a guttering candle, it was extremely difficult to see what I was reading.

L.E. Muir
Marmoset Breeders Association

"I loved him, dear reader, of course I did... but I loved his yeasty breath more."

EAU DE MARM'ITE
POUR FEMME

LOVE
HATE

THE NEW FRAGRANCE
BY UNE LÉVER

CHAPTER 5

ADVENTURES THROUGH HISTORY

0000

Humans discover the truth about Marmite – but it's goodbye to the Garden of Eden. In the words of Genesis: "And the serpent said unto Eve, 'Hath God said ye shall not eat of everything in the Garden?' And Eve said unto the serpent, 'We may eat of everything in the Garden. But of the jar which is in the midst of the Garden, God hath said Ye shall not eat of it, lest ye die.' And the serpent said unto Eve, 'Aw, go on! Die? Don't be daft. God just says that because He doesn't want you to know about Good and Evil.' So Eve did open the jar and did make a sandwich of the contents thereof, and she and Adam did eat said sandwich. And the eyes of both of them were opened, and they knew all about Good and Evil. So that was that for the day. " Clearly, they just loved Marmite. But God - whose attitude to yeast extract has never been firmly determined - stormed into the Garden soon afterwards, banished Adam and Eve to a problem housing estate and spirited away the serpent's legs. And that set the tone for what was to come.

500,000 BC

Groups of hunter-gatherers develop increasingly sophisticated ways of catching their prey. Archaeologists now believe this could be linked to the invention of ale-brewing in central Europe. At some stage in the period, brewing methods improved dramatically, thus leading to the first ever product (and by-product) surplus. Recent excavations in the Biergut Valley have revealed vast areas of fossilized yeast extract, in which there are the bones of mammoths, mastodons, aurochs, hartebeest, unicorns and other prehistoric mammals. Biergut Man seems to have dug pit traps perhaps 100 metres across and filled them with liquid Marmite. The large animals, drawn irresistibly by the yeasty aroma, plunged into the pits and were soon stuck fast. The hunters were able to slaughter them in huge numbers. Such events would certainly have been celebrated by week-long feasts of eating and drinking, as suggested by the discovery nearby of large piles of empty lager cans.

1323 BC

The boy pharaoh Tutankhamun is buried in a secret tomb in Egypt's Valley of the Kings. Around his gilded coffin are stacked treasures of all kinds, along with supplies to keep him going in the Afterlife – precious oils, fruit, nuts, crisps, mummified saveloys, bread (possibly for the making of toast, using the faience toasting fork provided) and an alabaster jar of Marmite. Three thousand years later, archaeologists crack the riddle of a hitherto mysterious black hieroglyph in the Royal Palace at Thebes: it shows, without a doubt, yeast extract. Inspired by this breakthrough, Howard Carter rediscovers the tomb. To his horror, all the ancient foodstuffs have rotted away, with one startling exception. The Marmite has been unaffected by the broiling desert heat. In celebration of his great find, Carter holds a grand afternoon tea in the tomb.

750 BC

On his long voyage home from Troy, Odysseus faces several stern challenges to his ingenuity. His survival and safe return home to Ithaca are due in no small part to the supply of Marmite given him by the goddess Athena. It proves to be as versatile as it is delicious. Dabbed liberally behind the ears, it saves Odysseus from being turned into a pig by Circe. Smeared on a pointed stake, it is used to blind the Cyclops when he traps them in a cave. When sailing past the Sirens, Odysseus stuffs the ears of his crew with compressed balls of Marmite sandwich, so they will not hear the seductive singing. James Joyce is later to make an oblique reference to this episode in his novel Ulysses, when Bloom offers his Marmite sandwich to a sailor in Doheny and Nesbitt's bar.

AD 50

One of the less well-known species of Roman gladiator was the miles extracticus (which roughly translates as "Marmite soldier"). Introduced by the Emperor Nero as a cunning tribute to his passion for soft-boiled eggs, this fighter was an instant hit at the Colosseum. His main weapon, an empty Marmite jar attached to a length of guttapercha, could be swung round to entangle

Marmite creates an unforseen divisive split in the early years

the legs of the opponent, or drawn taut and released to endanger the head and, on occasion, more intimate areas. The jar's contents, rubbed over the gladiator's naked body, made him hard to grapple with at close quarters. Extracticus was usually pitted against similarly spread-oriented gladiators, such as marmaladarius or the notorious female wielder of hazel-based confections, nutella. His fall was swift and inevitable, however, once the lions got their first lick.

AD 790

En route for Lindisfarne, a Viking raiding party is blown disastrously off course and lands at Goole. The planned programme of rape and pillage is hastily abandoned when the Norsemen discover a rude hut stacked to the rafters with Marmite. The recipe for this ancient spread has been painstakingly rediscovered during the Dark Ages by Saxon yeast craftsmen. It is a form of food hitherto unknown in Scandinavia, and the raiders gorge upon it ecstatically. A few go too far and become berserk in a fittingly Viking manner (the earliest recorded example of "Marmite Rage"). The local inhabitants – known as Goolies – sensibly flee to seek refuge in the nearby settlements of Pontefract and Knottingley, taking with them the secret of the extract's manufacture. For the next 90 years, the Vikings make countless expeditions to the same coastline in search of the ambrosial extract. They even land and build settlements. But all in vain.

1219

Genghis Khan and his mounted hordes sweep westwards across the Iranian Empire. One by one, great cities are left in smoking ruins, and the vast plateau is dotted with mountains of skulls. Terror stalks the land. Only one small settlement escapes the destruction. As news arrives of the Mongols' approach, the lord of the city of Mah-el-Meit decides on a daring ruse. He recalls the outsize load of yeast extract left behind, luckily, by a stricken caravan party the year before. He sees that – equally luckily – a sandstorm is on its way. In a blur of desperate activity, citizens are ordered to paint the contents of every Marmite jar over the outer walls of the town. Minutes later, the storm brings a blizzard of sand which sticks firmly to the walls, making them look just like

the surrounding desert. This camouflage completely fools Genghis Khan and his generals, who thunder past unseeing and disappear over the horizon.

1492

Christopher Columbus sails from Spain and heads west across the Atlantic. This bold move goes directly against the traditional explorers' advice, summed up in the ancient slogan "Go Ye East [or, in some accounts, "Yeast"] Young Man". He expects to hit China or Japan in a few days. Instead, after four weeks his sailors have seen no sign of land. They grow increasingly fretful at the vast emptiness about them, fearing they are about to sail off the edge of the world. Then, three days later, a lookout high in the rigging spies a tiny object bobbing off the port bow. Using his shrimping net, Columbus niftily hoists it aboard. It proves to be a black glass screwtop jar containing a scrap of paper with a scrawled message: "You are now entering American sea-space. No liquids, tweezers or sharp implements. Have a nice day." Columbus and his men realize to their joy that they are close to some form of civilization, and break out the sherry in celebration.

1503

Leonardo da Vinci and Michelangelo are each commissioned to paint a grand mural in the Palazzo Vecchio in Florence. Being bitter rivals as well as far from good friends, the competition is intense. Michelangelo begins sketching a gigantic battle scene on one wall and makes good progress. The famously laidback Leonardo arrives late and tries to catch up. He too sketches a gigantic battle scene, then immediately starts applying a special waxy undercoat of his own invention. This proves to be a disaster. The paints run off the undercoat and drip onto the floor. In desperation, Leonardo mixes a new concoction, incorporating random ingredients from his kitchen, including Marmite. Success is instantaneous. The paint holds its line and dries steadily, allowing Leonardo to pull ahead of his more careful rival. Seeing this, Michelangelo wrathfully flings down his brushes and stalks out, never to return. Leonardo wins! (Sadly, his great work survived only a few months before being destroyed by a plague of salt-hungry bats.)

Cavemen used Marmite tar pit traps to catch their tea.

N is for Nourishing
Marmite is an extraordinarily health-giving foodstuff for almost everyone, including pregnant women and anaemic children. See also Vitamin B.

O is for Olympics
Chinese authorities banned Vegemite from the 2008 Games, severely denting Australian morale. Meanwhile boxing gold medallist James de Gale referred to himself as 'The Marmite Man – people either love me or hate me.' Back in 1956, Marmite was a major sponsor of the British Olympic Team.

1560

Why did Queen Elizabeth I never marry? The answer may lie with a hitherto neglected incident at the beginning of her reign. The young queen was being pestered by many royal suitors, and decided to settle the matter with a grand contest. The suitors – including the King of Spain, Archduke Charles of Austria and Ivan the Terrible – had to compete against her in dancing, hunting, singing, drinking and eating. She would marry the first one to defeat her. The queen easily out-danced, out-hunted, out-sang and out-drank the men (even Ivan), and soon concluded they were a disappointing lot. It only remained for her to triumph at eating in order to avoid marrying any of them. She ordered that the feast should conclude with Marmite sandwiches, suspecting this would prove too much for her less than manly wooers. Her hunch proved correct. The competing princes were unable to chew even a mouthful, and slunk away humiliated to their distant thrones. Elizabeth, triumphantly dabbing up the final crumbs with a royal forefinger, now knew she would remain the Virgin Queen.

1665

Fleeing the plague which is ravaging Cambridge, Isaac Newton returns to his family's farm in Lincolnshire. Here he wanders about the hedgerows, pondering on the structure of the universe and working out complex mathematical formulae on the backs of pigs. When his father suggests that there is muck spreading to be done, Isaac replies that he is too busy inventing calculus. The young genius then spends hours in the barn fiddling about with bits of glass. His father mentions that the cows need milking, but Newton declines, on the grounds that he is splitting white light. He spends the whole of the next day sitting under an apple tree. His father asks him to weed the turnips, but Newton explains that he is puzzling out a theory of gravity. "I'll give thee gravity!" shouts his father, and throws the nearest handy object (in this case, a jar of Marmite) at the student's head. Shortly afterwards, Isaac Newton formulates his theory of gravitational attraction, and returns to Cambridge.

1773

Demonstrators dressed as Native Americans board British ships in Boston Harbour. In protest against the shocking Tea Tax being levied by the British, they empty the cargo of tea into the sea. This incident becomes celebrated as the Boston Tea Party, though of course it was not a party at all (there being no fairy cakes, ginger pop or Up Jenkins). What is less well-known is the Yonkers Marmite Party, a parallel action which takes place a few miles down the coast. Here, New Englanders dressed as pantomime dames (and also protesting against unjust taxes) board British ships and empty their cargo of yeast extract into the harbour. This has an astonishing threefold effect. The sea turns black. The sudden addition of several tons of such a tasty substance attracts vast shoals of mackerel, herring and cod, which are gratefully netted by the town's fishermen (two of whom become instant millionaires). And the threatened Marmite Tax is dropped, never to be heard of again.

1815

Napoleon, imprisoned on the island of Elba, is longing to escape. So many attempts have already failed – the tunnel (flooded), the rubbish cart dodge (he is too short to climb in) the helicopter (not yet invented) - that he is close to despair. Then his annual ration of Marmite arrives and a delighted Napoleon hurriedly opens a pot and dips in a finger. In his haste he smears some of the extract on his upper lip. His wife asks why he is covered in Marmite. Suddenly, inspiration strikes. "Not Marmite, Josephine," says Napoleon, pointing out that it is actually a false moustache. It will make him unrecognizable. Disguised as a hairy Italian fisherman, he crosses to the mainland, resumes his normal imperial garb and begins his march on Paris. But his adventure ends disastrously at the Battle of Waterloo and he is exiled again – this time to faraway St Helena. The Duke of Wellington forbids him the use of any form of savoury spread.

1666: Isaac Newton is brained by a falling Marmite fruit on his bonce

A most curious animal from Deepest Sumatra

Victorians used Marmite for pickling curiosities

1837

Isambard Kingdom Brunel masterminds the building of the Great Western Railway from London to Bristol. With unflagging energy he dashes off designs for every part of it - stations, bridges, tunnels, coaches, tea trollies, porters' watch chains, sandwich dispensers and speak-your-weight machines. One thing stumps him: the locomotives. How can he build something sturdy enough to hurtle along at unimagined speeds, yet handsome enough to be an instant design classic? For weeks he grapples with the problem, at his desk and at home. Then, one afternoon at the tea table, he fiddles fretfully with the condiments. His eye is caught by the random arrangement of containers and crockery. Butter dish… toast rack… swiss roll… Marmite jar! In an instant, he sees how these will fit together to form a dynamic and delightful solution for his steam locomotives (the top of the jar – unscrewed – will of course form the funnel). He rushes to his drawing board, and the legendary 0-6-2 "Black Spread" Class is born.

1867

Karl Marx publishes the first volume of his groundbreaking work Das Kapital, which lays the foundations for the spread of Communism. But the book sells very slowly. Penniless, the great thinker looks for another way of earning a living – one which sticks strictly to his socialist principles. He gets a part-time job in a London brewery, where he soon becomes fascinated with finding a use for the surplus yeast extract produced in beer-making. He bottles it and markets it as "Marx-mite: The Spread of Communism". Marx's stall becomes a familiar sight outside the British Library, and many literary figures buy his wares, including Anna Sewell (author of Black Beauty). Within months, he has earned enough to start work on the second volume of Kapital, and the extract business is abandoned. But Marx's achievements are to have a vast influence on later revolutionaries, including Simon Bovrilar (who launches Bovril), Mao Tse-tung (who launches "Mao-mite") and the Australian Les Veggie.

1879

The British Museum announces a state of emergency. For the past four decades, explorers have been sending back a flood of exotic specimens from remote corners of the world - birds, butterflies, fish, snakes, animal skins, shrunken heads (and other human parts), slugs, spiders and several tons of bat guano. This has caused major problems (especially when the fish were sent by post from Tierra del Fuego). The store rooms of the Museum are stacked with mountains of the stuff, now catastrophically rotting. All kinds of preservatives have been tried, from brine to vintage madeira, but nothing seems to halt the putrefaction of these priceless items. Queen Victoria is consulted on the matter. She in turn asks her old standby, the Duke of Wellington, what can be used to save the specimens. The ancient Duke (now equipped with ill-fitting dentures) apparently mutters: "Marmite, ma'am".

1896

The first Modern Olympic Games are held in Athens. They are the brainchild of the Baron de Coubertin, who believes that "the essential thing is not to have conquered but to have fought well". But not everything runs smoothly. The swimming events have to take place in the sea, because no-one has built a pool. The wrestling final goes on so long that it is halted because of nightfall. The rowing events are cancelled due to high winds. And many sports are dropped due to lack of space or interest. One which survives the cut is indoor Marmite jar rolling (the object being to roll an empty jar the greatest distance). This sport, which had grown up in the temperance halls of Manchester (as a demonstration of the peaceful possibilities of yeast), is almost unknown outside England. It promises a certain medal sweep for the British team. But on the day an unfancied Greek athlete, Spyridon Extractopoulos, produces a freak roll of 94 yards (wind-assisted) to carry off the gold. After this humiliation, jar rolling quickly loses popularity in the UK, though it is still played in the remoter areas of the Peloponnese.

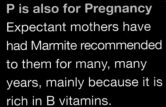

P is also for Pregnancy
Expectant mothers have had Marmite recommended to them for many, many years, mainly because it is rich in B vitamins.

P is for Paddington Bear
Paddington appeared in a 2007 TV commercial for Marmite, and shocked some viewers by abandoning his beloved marmalade sandwiches.

P is also for Pasteur, Louis (1822-1895)
The famed French chemist was the first to realize that yeast cells were part of living plants, each possessing a well defined and complex structure.

P is also for Pernicious Anaemia, a condition that Marmite was most 'efficacious in the treatment of', so reported a 1932 edition of *The Lancet*. All down to its high Vitamin B content, don't you know.

1923

John Logie Baird moves to a rented room in Hastings. His previous projects – creating diamonds by electricity, making specially thick socks for walkers, and finding an improved method for bottling mango jam – having all failed, he has been advised to seek a quiet life by the sea. But he is soon bored, and decides to invent television. Suitable materials are hard to find, so Baird improvises. He assembles a tea chest, a biscuit tin, an electric motor from a toy train, two knitting needles, a black pudding, a box of collar stiffeners, a mole wrench and five yards of knicker elastic. One thing is missing. Somewhere he must find a round hollow object - possibly three inches high - made of (preferably) darkened glass, with a screw top. Rooting through his landlord's kitchen shelves, he finds the very thing. Quickly rinsing out the contents, he bolts the jar in place and completes his first TV set. His landlord, unfortunately, is enraged at the loss of his Marmite, and evicts Baird on the spot.

1959

After overthrowing Cuba's rightwing dictator in a Communist revolution, Fidel Castro becomes the island's new leader. This immediately makes him a leading hate figure of the USA. Over the next four decades the CIA and other bodies make more than 600 attempts to assassinate Castro. They try everything – exploding cigars, Mafia hitmen, poisoned cold cream, snipers, bomb-filled molluscs, diving suits infected with skin disease, excruciatingly tight camouflage trousers – but each one ends in humiliating failure.. How does El Comandante manage to survive? A large part of the answer lies with the widespread Cuban hatred of Marmite. Castro never travels without a jar of this product near him. He knows none of his close aides will ever touch it, but that a foreigner – especially an American – will find it impossible to resist. Therefore, a daily check will alert him to the presence of a possible assassin. He even has a saying: "Marmito robado – gringo amenazado" ("Marmite stolen – Yankee threat").

1967

John Lennon arrives at Abbey Road studios with an idea for a new song called All You Need is Marmite. He wants the Beatles to record it in a live TV broadcast, accompanied by the London Symphony Orchestra, the Dagenham Girl Pipers, the Glasgow Orpheus Choir, the late Frank Crumit, the Memphis Jug Band, and Wilson, Keppel and Betty. Producer George Martin is sceptical. He points out that the message of the lyrics hardly chimes in with the peace and love spirit of the times. He especially objects to the line: "Eleanor Rigby, eating some Marmite she keeps in a jar by the door". All the same, the recording eventually goes ahead (though with slightly reduced backing), to immense acclaim. However, the BBC later feels uneasy about product placement and employs Richard Burton to overdub the word "Marmite" with "love" throughout. On release, it races to Number One.

1969

Eagle, the lunar module of Apollo 11, touches down on the moon. Astronauts Neil Armstrong and Buzz Aldrin emerge and immediately set to work. For two and a half hours they unload a mountain of scientific equipment, collect rock samples, plant a US flag, take photos and bounce around a lot. They leave a plaque bearing the signatures of Richard Nixon and Elvis Presley, plus a goodie bag containing a gold replica of an olive branch (which would, of course, be instantly recognizable to any passing alien) and a plastic replica of a McMuffin. By this time, naturally, both men are pretty peckish, so they return to the Eagle for lunch. As they munch, Armstrong and Aldrin check that all is ready for takeoff. They find to their horror that the launch button has seized up, thanks to a mishap with some moon dust. The pair try everything, to no avail. Finally, Armstrong seizes his colleague's half-finished Marmite sandwich and applies it vigorously to the button. The engine fires, the module soars aloft and they escape from the moon. The journey back to Earth is tense, however, and Armstrong and Aldrin do not speak to each other for forty years.

1969: Neil Armstrong uses Buzz Aldrin's Marmite sandwich to lubricate a wonky fuel injector piston on the lunar lander, thus enabling them to escape the moon. The journey back is tense and neither speak for another 40 years.

Q is for Queen
The royal party visited
the Marmite factory in
Burton-on-Trent during
Elizabeth II's Jubilee
year in 2002.

CHAPTER 6

MARMITE

A CULTURAL
PHENOMENON

THE LAST TEA by Leonardo da Vitamin (1452–1519)

The painting depicts, from left to right: Bartholomew still in his wetsuit, James and Andrew who have clearly had just about as much Marmite as they can take and Judas, never to be seen without his typewriter, whilst Peter leans behind him and gives John a vicious Karate chop to the throat, breaking his neck instantly. In the centre Jesus of Niacin shields his going-away present and displays his joy at the thought of the sticky moments ahead. Then there is Thomas, without doubt showing his displeasure at not having been given a similar present, James demonsating the position that his leader is likely to be adopting the following day and Philip, beginning to remove his clothes. Beside them are Matthew and Simon who are about to attempt to remove Jesus's troublesome wisdom tooth with a transparent rope. Jude Thiamin leans in between them and prepares to shout 'Pull'. Interestingly, the painting demonstrates clearly how too much yeast can dissolve your eyelids.

X-RAY TECHNOLOGY CLEARLY
REVEALS LEONARDO'S FIRST
DRAFT OF THE MONA LISA
AND SUGGESTS A REASON
FOR THE MOST ENIGMATIC
SMILE IN ART HISTORY.

R is for Repellent
Many travellers swear by Marmite's surprising insect-repelling properties. Some believe it is connected to the ingestion of B vitamins.

R is also for Riboflavin
Otherwise known as Vitamin B2, this is a handy nutrient and health promoter in humans. It plays a key role in metabolizing fats, proteins and carbohydrates.

R is also for
Rice Cakes A new Marmite-flavoured product launched in 2007.

R is also for Roast potatoes
Can be transformed with a light coating of Marmite before cooking.

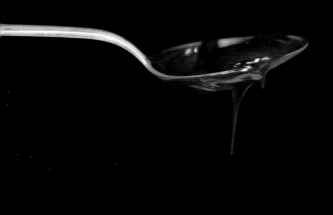

DARK SIDE OF THE SPOON

NEVER MIND
THE BOVRIL

HERE'S THE

Yeasts Away!

From the memoirs of Pilot Officer Rob O'Flavin

We'd been training for months, of course, under a cloak of the utmost secrecy. The exact nature of the large round brown object that was slung beneath each of our aircraft was not known, but it was obviously some sort of bomb. We'd dropped them time and again and now we were to do it for real. I was with my usual crew: Bill the bomb-aimer, Johnny the flight engineer, navigator Peter and Dick on his wireless. Up above in the mid turret was Bunty and, out on his own at the rear, Ted: at 18, although I suspected he was younger, the baby of the team.

Having flown out over the North Sea, we had turned to the South towards the target. It had, so far, been a long and uneventful trip; a little boring perhaps but that was something for which to be grateful. Suddenly my headphones crackled into action, "Skipper?". It was young Ted.
"Yes Ted?"
"Are we nearly there yet?"
We were still more than two hours away.
"No Ted, why?"
"I'm bored".
"Well think of something to keep you occupied"
"OK Skip".

The line went dead. We carried on serenely. It was a cloudless night and the full moon gave an eerie light. I could see other aircraft all around me. My earphones crackled once more. I again recognised Ted's voice.

'Just then the aircraft shook violently and tracer flew through the cockpit'

"I spy, with my little eye, something beginning with M".
I was pleased that Ted had taken my advice. I would humour him.
"Is it the Moon?"
"No"
"Is it a Microphone?"
"No"
"Is it a....?"
Just then the aircraft shook violently and tracer flew through the cockpit. I heard Bunty and Ted letting rip and immediately corkscrewed left and dropped several thousand feet before levelling out. There was no further attack. I seemed to have shaken off our assailant.
"No, it was a Messerschmitt"
"Thank you Ted, I'd worked that out. No more games, you bloody fool, and keep yours eyes peeled."

We flew on, a little chastened, scanning the sky for the slightest shadow. I had sent Johnny aft to check for damage and he came back to report that the bomb had taken a hit. A small quantity of thick brown liquid had seeped out, which he had mopped up. His gloves were covered in it.
"It doesn't look too bad, but we'd better keep an eye on it", he told me. I asked him to check every ten minutes or so and he resumed his position. Ted, however, was still restless.
"Skipper?"
"Yes Ted?"
"I'm really hungry".
We needed to keep our energy levels up so I asked Johnny to break open the pack of sandwiches which we always brought with us and take some back to the youngster. At least, with luck, he won't talk with his mouth full, I thought to myself. A few minutes later Ted had obviously left his microphone switched on.

"Yuck! Aarrgh! These are horrid!"

"What's the matter Ted?"

"Johnny's smeared some brown muck on my sandwiches and they taste horrid. I hate them"

"I'm afraid that's your problem, Ted, now get on with it."

The target was in sight now and I sent Bill to arm the bomb. A quick twist of the yellow cap and we were ready. Dropping down to sixty feet we all slipped into automatic mode and we were thankful that our hours of training came to the fore.

There was a jar as the bomb slipped away and everything went as planned until we pulled up after our run and flew over the crest of a hill. The starboard engine was hit by flak and immediately caught fire, The aircraft faltered and nearly stalled. I dropped the nose and managed to bring things back under control just as we were skimming the tree tops. Meanwhile Johnny had succesfully operated the fire extinguishers. Phew, that was close!.

"Skipper"

"Yes?"

"I feel sick"

"Shut up, Ted!"

As we climbed and turned for home I looked back and saw the results of our night's work. The whole valley was covered in a thick brown morass. Cars and trains had ground to a sticky halt. Buildings were engulfed. The whole valley seemed to have been paralysed. It had been a success.

Pushing the throttles fully forward, Peter gave me a course and we ran for home. There were no fighters to interrupt our progress: Dick had heard that they had all stuck to their airfields. With much relief we crossed the Channel.

"Skipper"

"Yes, Ted"

"I need a wee".

'The target was in sight now... a quick twist of the yellow cap and we were ready'

S is for Stink
Which probably needs no explanation at all.

S is also for Shakespeare,
The Bard used yeast as a figure of speech in his plays. In *Macbeth*, he describes how 'the yeasty waves confound and swallow navigation up'. The substance also gets a walk-on part in *Hamlet* and *The Winter's Tale*.

S is also for Shortage
of Marmite Yeast – and therefore Marmite – supplies were seriously stretched soon after the outbreak of World War Two in 1939. There was a huge surge in demand for the extract, resulting in the plea added to advertisements: "Use Marmite Sparingly".

S is also for Soldiers
Strips of toast (or bread), butter and marmite cut exactly to allow the eater to dip them into an opened boiled egg.

S is also for Spreading
The best method of getting Marmite onto your toast or sandwich.

It was that evening, whilst showering and glancing over to the note that had been slipped under the door by the kindly proprietor of the Bates Motel, that Marion Crane lost both her composure and her soap on a rope.

COMPLIMENTARY MARMITE-TOASTED BREAKFAST
FREE WITH EVERY NIGHT'S STAY AT THE BATES MOTEL.

T is for Taxis
In its centenary year of 2002, Marmite emblazoned a fleet of London taxis with the Marmite livery.

T is also for Thiamin
A soluble form of the Vitamin B1 which is vital in the prevention of some deficiency diseases, and in the general promotion of health. It is, of course, present in Marmite.

U is for Umami
The so-called 'fifth taste', which is detected by sensors on the human tongue. It is named with the Japanese word meaning 'tasty' or 'savoury'. It occurs naturally in many foods, including Marmite.

U is also for Urgggh
The reaction of a Marmite-hater on accidentally eating a Marmite sandwich. (See *Hate*).

Week 38, September 2009

£2.96

Yeast Weekly

Your fortnightly fermentation news: now every week!

Win your own weight in single-celled fungi in our prize crossword competition

Also in this weeks issue...

6 Top Tips to get this seasons yeasty look

READERS TRUE STORY

'My yeasty lust shame with hubby's best friend'

We meet Ron Lump and discover the lost art of Marmity bowls

The lost art of Marmity bowls

A special report by John Henry Dixon

For many hundreds of years the sleepy village of Stooge Bogle has been little talked about and seldom in the news, Until now, that is. Last week saw the unearthing of the only-known example of a particular type of sixteenth century bowling green. Few knew that the village was the headquarters of an arcane game all those years ago. Ron Lump, the organist at the village church of St. Rewth was one who did. I met Ron this week and asked him how this came about. He takes up the story:

'In olden days days no self-respecting community would be without a Marmity bowling team'

'I have always been interested in reintroducing old sports and pastimes to modern society' said Ron. 'There are so many that should not be lost in the mists of time. In South Wales I was the first man for over a hundred years to take part in Mine Shouting and they now run a very keen pub league. In Norfolk we brought back Chicken Juggling to the local people and elsewhere we have recreated a following for Shrapnel Chasing, Worm Blending and Mouse Welding. These, of course, are games of varying antiquity but ones which I firmly believe can be enjoyed afresh by generation upon generation of sporting and hobbying enthusiasts.

'You can imagine my excitement, therefore, after I kept hearing stories of the local schoolchildren getting cuts and grazes whilst playing football on the school pitch. Mysteriously the injuries were almost invariably caused by small shards of brown glass. It set me thinking and the seed of an idea took root in my mind. Surely not? Yes, something told me that this just could be the long-lost site of the legendary Marmity Hollow. I was given permission to excavate the pitch in the summer holidays and in no time at all I was proved right. A near-perfect sixteenth century Marmity Green was still there, along with several intact Marmity Bowls, or "Chars" as they were known, and, of course, a number of broken ones which had caused the injuries in the first place that led me to this discovery.'

'In olden days no self-respecting community would be without a Marmity bowling team and this remained the case for two centuries. Its decline came quite suddenly and the last match was recorded on the Isle of Lewis in 1803. The game itself is highly skilful and is best described as Crown Green bowling in reverse. The green is a hollow with the lowest point in the centre. A small white ball, the "Shack" is rolled first and, as one would expect, it eventually stops at the centre of the hollow. The aim now is to roll your Char so that is the one which finishes furthest from the Shack, whilst remaining within the confines of the Hollow. This is extremely difficult as the natural tendency is for gravity to

pull them towards the Shack. The skill comes from manipulating your Char so that it rolls onto its "Yealtip", a flat circular area at its top, and stops.'

Ron then went into a deconstruction of the technique of the game which I have to admit I found a little confusing, but his passion was unmistakable and it almost brought a lump to my throat. Would this passion spread to others and begin the return of the game to its former pre-eminence? I pressed Ron on this point, 'Well, I hope so. I've always managed to enthuse others with these ancient contests. I admit the Worms were a little slow to catch on but I have no doubt that, provided people are prepared to dig accurately, within a very short space of time Marmite Bowling will be the talk of the town.' At this point Ron's mobile phone rang, 'What, really? A genuine Treacle Pit? Right, I'm leaving now'. And with that he made his excuses and left. Clearly, for Ron, the resurrection of ancient sports is an unending quest.

Ron Lump: a man with a passion for reviving long-neglected sports and pastimes back into modern society.

Ma might...

Each week, our resident agony aunt tries to answer your yeasty conundrums. This week...

I dabbled in a nibble of hubby's best friend's nuts and fear I'll now be nobbled!

Q

Dear Ma,

Several weeks ago, in celebration of his appointment to a new position at work, my husband Ken invited close friends and relatives round for a few drinks and nibbles. Many glasses of Languedoc Chardonnay and Ken's famed planter punch later and all were in high spirits. On the coffee table that had been pushed out from the centre of the room to sit next to the Queen Anne wing chair, lay empty plates and bowls on raffia mats. The canapés and treats I had arranged there earlier that day had been demolished in a matter of minutes.

With all merry and inebriated, I slipped away to the kitchen to make a start on the washing up. I had just begun to work a lather with my pan scourer when Terry, my husband's best friend, entered carrying a cluster of the last of my nutty brittle. He asked to what did it owe its piquant tang and I duly revealed all (my first mistake). He then asked had I ever considered replacing the quarter-teaspoon of salt with a full

'There then followed a moment of weakness... a moment of madness.'

heaped teaspoon of Marmite Yeast Extract? I was taken aback. Seeing me all of a dither he pounced, adding: 'If you wish, I could offer you a taste of the alternative right here and now?' I must have nodded my consent (my second mistake), for he then revealed a piece that he had been stowing in his trouser pocket throughout the course of the party. There then followed a moment of weakness... a moment of madness. With my mouth agape, he pushed that warm salty cluster of nuts fully inside me. I would be lying if I said I didn't enjoy it (I did) but immediately after it was over I felt a deep sense of shame coupled with a quite violent though curiously not-unpleasant gagging reflex.

Twenty-seven calendar days have now passed and my betrayal feels as painful today as it did in those regrettable few seconds after the scene in the kitchen. Ken has an abhorrent dislike of Marmite which dates back to his childhood. Mindful of this, I'd never really felt the need to give it a try myself. But now that I have been tempted by Terry, I don't half have a hankering to try it again. I'm confused and truly don't know what to do. Can you help?

Yours, in desperation,

Mrs E. Trimball, Dungeness

'...I don't half have a hankering to try it again.'

'...you must decide whether you can do without this thrill in your life'

Ma might just know the answer to your predicament, Mrs Trimball – and what a very troubling predicament it must be for you!

Has Terry waved his nuts under your nose since that day, I wonder? Or is it an inner demon with which you find yourself battling? If the former, then you need to decide whether there is some unfinished business between the two of you to attend to – and if there is, I would recommend a frank and open discussion immediately. If the latter, you must decide whether you can do without this thrill in your life – and if the answer is you can't, then I wonder if you could perhaps try talking your husband round to giving it a go once more after all these years? If it so happens that he still doesn't agree with it perhaps he might at least be able to consider a compromise that would allow you to enjoy once more the taste of Terry's nuts whilst he finds pleasure in those which he knows and trusts? If your husband should agree to this, and a salty offering is still there on the table from Terry, it might then be that you can manage to please both men whilst getting a little something for yourself too. I sincerely hope you manage to pull it off, as it were, since doing so will surely testify to the great strength and trust you have in your relationship.

And I do hope your husband has settled into his new job well.

With my best yeasty wishes,

Ma

UNLEASH THE YEAST GODDESS IN YOU

Hey Girls, are you bored of those bright, garish colours heaped on from lid to brow? You know – the ones that look like your granny's piled them on with a trowel! Well, fear not! There's only one colour to be seen in this season and that colour is BROWN. We run you through a few yeasty tones and show you how with careful blending and even application you can achieve a delicious look! This great selection of shades will help spruce up and dull down the look – read on and extract all you can to get the look!

Smear on the smoulder
Use these great shades to create smouldering spumy eyes (see 6 Steps, opposite). Try Eastern Yeast (left) from **£6**, or the fab duo (right), Beige Barm and Fermented Brown at **£13**. Both YST.

Spread over blemishes
We all suffer the odd blemish, but this great concealer by Scarmite covers all spots without looking caked on. **£10.95**

Lickable lips
Take yeasty beauty to the next level with these mucky brown shades, new from the Kiss-Me-Sick Lips range in 'choke' and 'puke' colours. **£12**

6 Steps to *smouldering* eyes

1 Use a base

Use an eyeshadow primer for a great base to smear on underneath your eyeshadow to allow easy spreading. **Use a liquid yeast base to stop your eyeshadow melting into your eyelid crease. Keep those eyes smouldering all day!**

2 Line the eye

Use brown eyeliner for a less harsh look than black and give the effect of larger eyes. Apply above the upper lashes and draw the line thicker in the middle if you want to affect the look of widening the eye. **Dab with a yeast-based sealant.**

3 Smudge

A key smokey look is to use the 'smudge' effect. You get this great look by using a lighter eyeliner under the lower lash line and 'smudging it', to give a soft smouldering look. **Use powdered yeast to feather a fine smudge.**

4 Base colour

Use a lighter base colour and pair it with a murkier hue and you'll be heading for that sultry, smokey look. **Use a base-coat of light-coloured yeast.**

5 Blend

With base and liner on you now need that smeared effect. Take the darker of your two shades and a large eyeshadow brush and blend colour into the lash line so that the eyeliner disappears. **Accentuate with a wipe of yeast gel.**

6 Finish off

To finish off the look, apply layers of volumising mascara. **For a final flourish, upturn a bucket of raw yeast over your head and continue to ferment for the remainder of the weekend.**

Tips
Remember to keep lips nude. When applying strong makeup, put the focus on either eyes or lips, never both.

Reader's Question

There are many weird and wonderful lengths that people will go to when it comes to hair conditioning – beer baths and raw-egg rubs to name but a couple. One of our readers, though, wonders if there is a yeasty alternative....

Q: I sweep hair at my local salon. Pam, a stylist at the salon, told me that a certain yeast-based product applied to my hair overnight will better nourish my locks than any normal leave-in conditioner could possibly do. Is this true and where can I get it? Also, is it true that Alopecia is a group of islands in the Pacific Ocean? Pam insists it is, but I think she might be pulling my pinkies! **Sarah, Staines**

A: Thanks for your letter, Sarah. It is indeed true. Yeast-based products are well known for their high vitamin content – great for conditioning lacklustre mops. There are, however, two notable side-effects. One is the abominable smell which is likely to require removing bed partners, animals and all naked flames from the house for a minimum period of 36 hours. The other is the extremely polarized results involved with each new virgin attempt: success or ruin; you will either love or hate the results. If you love it, you should probably endeavour to repeat the process each morning in lieu of breakfast. Marmite works particularly well (or very badly, of course) and can be picked up in most good high-street salons and chemists. Oh, and I regret your pinkies have probably suffered a good old tug! **Marie, Beauty Editor**

Puzzle Marmania

Kitchen Chaos!
Can you Spot the
5 differences?

WIN!
Spot the 5 differences
and be in with a chance
of winning an annual
subscription to
Yeast Weekly!

For your chance to
win these great
prizes, send all
entries to: PO BOX
328, Burton-on-Trent
Staffordshire

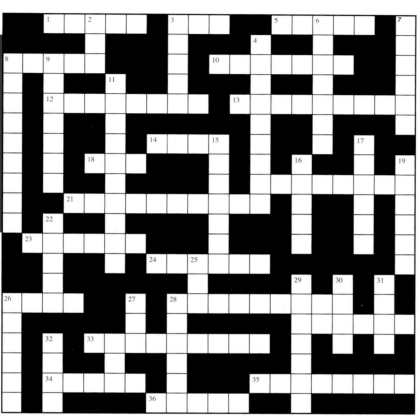

ACROSS

1. Grilled bread (5)
3. Fisherman lures his lover (4)
5. Our daily ___? (5)
8. Consistency of Marmite (5)
10. Love it or hate it (7)
12. Riboflavin and Niacin are forms of ? (8)
13. Low-fat alternative to butter (9)
14. Glass vessels that store yeast extract (4)
18. Seal 14 across with one of these (3)
20. Lunchtime snack (8)
21. An element integral to a recipe (10)
23. Submarine colour for top of jar (6)
24. Applying of Marmite (5)
26. Opposite of love (4)
28. Craving type of tendency (9)
33. Paddington's soft toy form (9)
34. A distinctly sodium-chloride-like flavour (5)
35. Savoury biscuits eaten with cheese (8)
36. To administer food (5)

DOWN

2. Eat in the past tense (3)
3. The colour of yeast extract (5)
4. The mealtime of boiled egg and soldiers (9)
6. Marmite is a yeast _____ (6)
7. Dairy spread for toast (6)
8. Nine-month spell right in folic acid (9)
9. The umami quality of yeast extract (7)
11. TV bear who ditched honey for Marmite (10)
15. Extract the most from malleable tube (7)
16. Implement for spreading Marmite on toast (5)
17. Fried pieces of savoury potato (6)
19. Perfect for crackers, biscuits and with wine (6)
22. The extract Marmite comes from (5)
25. Colour of the Bovril jar wrapper (3)
26. A world in the clouds (6)
27. Feed in the past tense (3)
28. The singular form of everyone (6)
29. Needed by the body for good health (7)
30. Opposite of 26 across (4)
31. Wax lyrical about wonder of yeast (4)
32. Posh rhyme equals slang word for food (4)

LOOKING to MEET

STICKY-FINGERED lover of dark stuff seeks similar for fun times. **Box no 27152**

DARK MAN with yeasty breath seeks kind or olfactorily-inferior woman. **Box no 20011**

GOOD TIMES GIRL seeks bad man to smear and lick and to be licked and smeared. **Box no 46462**

BUTTER-FINGERED BABE seeks strong man with safe pair of hands. **Box no 32582**

HUNGRY MALE looking for buxom female to saté appetite. **Box no 27990**

FORGETFUL yeast enthusiast wishes to find friendship and spectacles. **Box no 79521**

ARDENT ALLITERATOR after action, adventure and affectionate attention. Available? **Box no 63558**

FORGETFUL yeast enthusiast wishes to find friendship and spectacles. **Box no 79521**

BOVRIL BEAUTY looking to meat veggie alternative, give things a try and then take stock. **Box no 69289**

FORTY-SOMETHING attractive woman will try anything once and most things twice. Box no 24290

MATURE CHEESE LOVER seeking biscuit eater with dry scents of hummous. **Box no 11145**

TOP BIT OF CRUMPET looking for lover of Champagne to assist with toasting. **Box no 39915**

Anything yeasty considered. **Box 85544**

HORNY HERB GROWER looking to spice up her life. No thyme wasters, please. **Box 52298**

MAN WITH DARK SECRET wants to share it. **Box 23358**

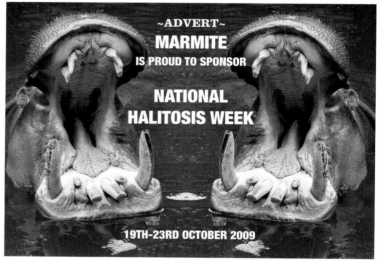

~ADVERT~
MARMITE IS PROUD TO SPONSOR
NATIONAL HALITOSIS WEEK
19TH–23RD OCTOBER 2009

DIFFIDENT, DYSLEXIC lady seeks uninhabited man. **Box no 46002**

ANAGRAM ENTHUSIAST seeks similar for Ram time. **Box 26574**

BUFFET-LOVING LADY looking for a a good spread. **Box 55628**

FUN-LOVING MALE wants to meet for a jar.

MALE WITH MARMITE and two left feet seeks female with Cup-final tickets. Please send photo of tickets. **Box 95527**

TOAST AND BUTTER looking for close companionship. **Box 52247**

MUSHROOM COLLECTOR looking for yellow caps. **Box 52289**

LOOKING to MEET

WANTED
PLAYERS FOR
BURTON-ON-TRENT
MARMITY
BOWLS TEAM

DIAL '0800 MARMITY'

ASK FOR RON

MARMITE FAN with good sense of smell and fun, seeks dominant friend for brown-nosing. **Box 54228**

GOOD-LOOKING male seeks girl with big yeasts. **Box 44859**

GIRL WITH BIG JAR seeks man with large spoon. **Box 56687**

ANAGRAM FANATIC searching for vole. **Box 20004**

YEAST MAN looking for his yeast woman. Rise up and be counted! **Box 10299**

EXCEEDINGLY UGLY MAN keen to be fixed up with blind date. **Box 77551**

BEEFY MAN of superior stock seeks spring chicken with whom to make perfect stew. **Box 41059**

LORRY HIJACKED. Marmite consignment stolen. Have you seen any of these?: Box 54807, Box 54812, Box 54823, Box 54834, Box 54846, Box 54847, Box 54867, Box 54877, Box 54882, Box 54889, Box 54102, Box 54125, Box 54133. Reward offered. **Box 54827**

YEASTY-BREATHED MAN seeks woman with very low self-esteem. **Box 32209**

MARMITE SOLDIER fit and ready for action. **Box 61011**

SOS! Confused bachelor seeks help resolving dating acronyms. **Box 34091**

LITTLE MISS TOASTIE looking for her Mr. Marmite. **Box 23254**

LOST: Yellow lid. Last seen during picnic outside Staines. Reward. **Box 44785**

MAD HATTER looking for friends for tea parties. **Box 98787**

HORNY MUM-TO-BE seeks regular supply of phallic acid. **Box 80122**

THE FOUR TOPS. I already have red, blue and green. Will collect. **Box 35568**

SECRETIVE SORT seeks classifieds information. **Box 75331**

MAN OF SIMPLE NEEDS seeks sex. **Box 71200**

CHAPTER 7

A DARK AND
DIRTY WORLD

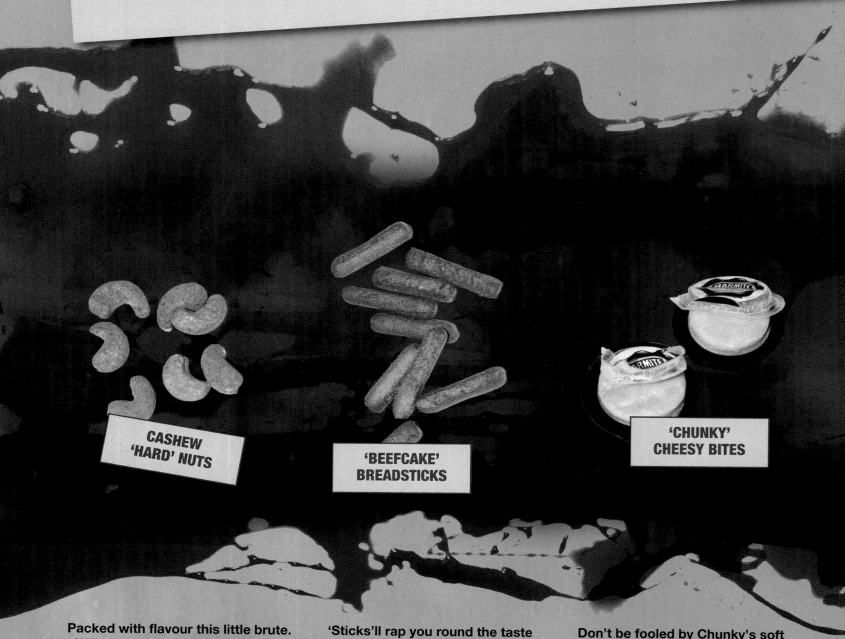

CASHEW 'HARD' NUTS

'BEEFCAKE' BREADSTICKS

'CHUNKY' CHEESY BITES

Packed with flavour this little brute. Will hit your taste buds good and hard and leave a piquant tang around your gums for a long time afterwards.

'Sticks'll rap you round the taste regions with a good smack and then – bang-bang! – come back and finish you off with another one-two.

Don't be fooled by Chunky's soft exterior: he'll still manage to leave a very nasty taste in your pie hole. You've been warned.

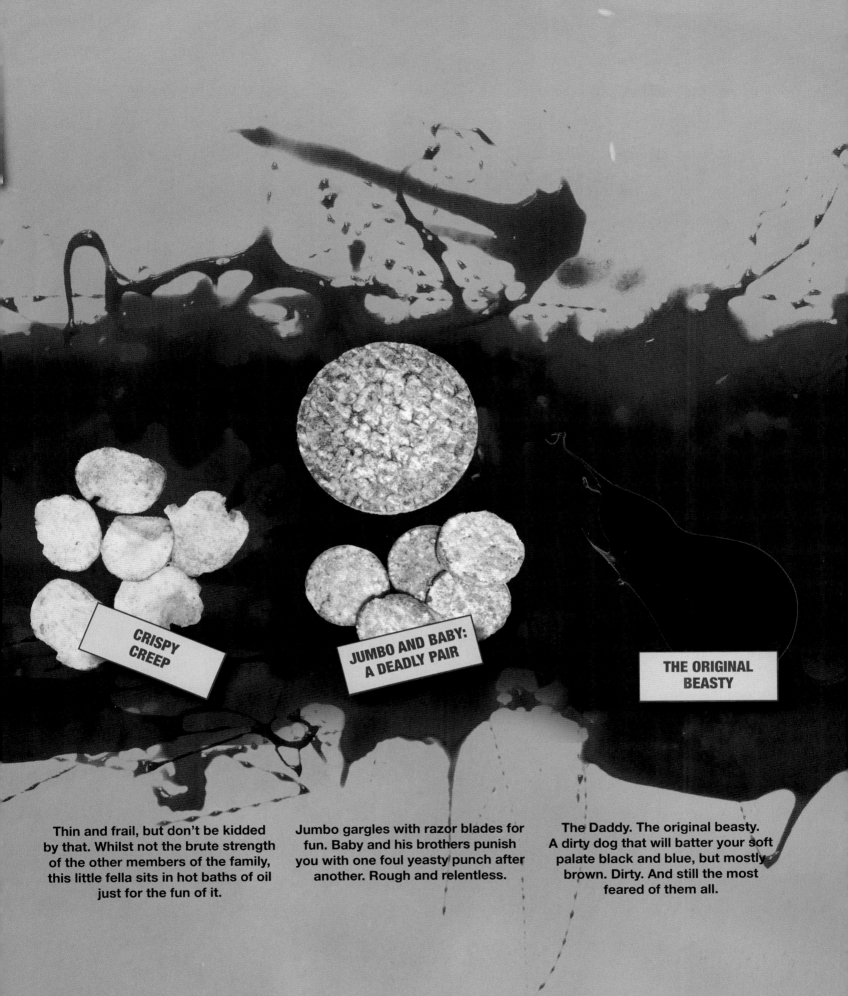

CRISPY CREEP

JUMBO AND BABY: A DEADLY PAIR

THE ORIGINAL BEASTY

Thin and frail, but don't be kidded by that. Whilst not the brute strength of the other members of the family, this little fella sits in hot baths of oil just for the fun of it.

Jumbo gargles with razor blades for fun. Baby and his brothers punish you with one foul yeasty punch after another. Rough and relentless.

The Daddy. The original beasty. A dirty dog that will batter your soft palate black and blue, but mostly brown. Dirty. And still the most feared of them all.

V is for Vegetarian
Non-meat eaters can indulge happily in Marmite, as it is an entirely vegetable product and is approved by the Vegetarian Society.

V is also for Vitamin B
Pioneering scientific analysis of Marmite in the early 20th century found that it was an excellent source of Vitamin B. Later research found that there was in fact a complex of B vitamins. These include B12 (essential for keeping our blood, bone marrow and nervous system in good shape), B1 (for a healthy nervous system and digestion), and B2 (for healthy skin and enzyme regulation).

V is also for Vegemite
Believed by most experts to be vastly inferior to Marmite.

W is for Wartime
Marmite was put into soldiers' ration packs during World War One, and used in POW camps as a dietary supplement in World War Two.

**W is also for
Westwood, Vivienne**
The acclaimed fashion pioneer and punk goddess designed a Marmite tee-shirt to celebrate the spread's centenary in 2002.

**W is also for
Wissler, Frederick**
One of the founders of the Marmite Food Extract Company (along with George Huth) in 1902.

WE CAN HELP

DON'T SUFFER ALONE

MILLIONS OF PEOPLE LOVE AND HATE.
BUT DID YOU KNOW THAT THERE ARE
A FEW WHO SIMPLY 'DON'T MIND'?

[WE KNOW, IT'S *WRONG.*]

IF YOU ARE ONE OF THEM,
IF YOU KNOW ONE OF THEM,
OR IF YOU JUST NEED TO TALK:
WE CAN HELP.

REMEMBER

THE SNIFF-LICK QUICK CHECK:

1 SNIFF
WHAT RESPONSE IS THERE?
A LOVER WILL SALIVATE AND NOT BE ABLE TO RESIST
LICKING LIPS.
A HATER WILL GAG AND RUN.

2 LICK
WHAT RESPONSE IS THERE?
ALL OTHER SENSES WILL TEMPORARILY SHUT DOWN.
RAPID-FIRE LOADING OF TOASTER WILL COMMENCE.
A HATER WILL GAG AND RUN.

MARMITE
AGNOSTICS
ANONYMOUS

WE CAN HELP

X is for Xtreme
Sandwiching Competition
Back in 2003, all you had to
do was send in a photo of
yourself with a Marmite jar
or sandwich in a bizarre
situation to stand the
chance of winning holiday
vouchers or a camera.

10 Marmite Near-Misses

1. **Marmite Mozzarella** (people either loved or grated it) 2. Marmite Paint Stripper (didn't shift the paint... best to gloss over its failings) 3. **Marmite Toothpaste** (failed to whiten teeth and retired many a brush too early) 4. Marmite Air Freshener (replaced all bad smells with one very bad smell) 5. **Marmite Upholstery Cleaner** (left its mark... a bit of a problem) 6. Marmite Floor Polish (lethally slippery... rubbed everyone up the wrong way) 7. **Marmite Engine Lubricant** (piston broke... aren't we all?) 8. Marmite Woodworking Filler (stayed soft... went against the grain) 9. **Marmite Eye Shadow** (made the eyes water and caused some funny looks) 10. Marmite-Flavoured Condoms (people could neither love nor mate with it)

Y is for Yeast
A huge family of one-celled fungi which can reproduce at an astonishing rate. They can also ferment carbohydrates, turning them into carbon dioxide and alcohol. Brewing yeast is the utterly essential ingredient in making beer.

Y is also for Yellow
The unmistakeable colour of the Marmite lid – once metal, now plastic.

Y is also for Yeats, William Butler
Irish poet whose surname was an anagram of yeast.

Z is for Zippy
A famously greedy and loudmouthed character from the children's TV show Rainbow, Zippy appeared in a 2002 commercial for Marmite. He was rendered speechless for once after biting into a Marmite sandwich.

Z is also for Zymurgy
The branch of chemistry concerned with the fermentation processes in brewing.

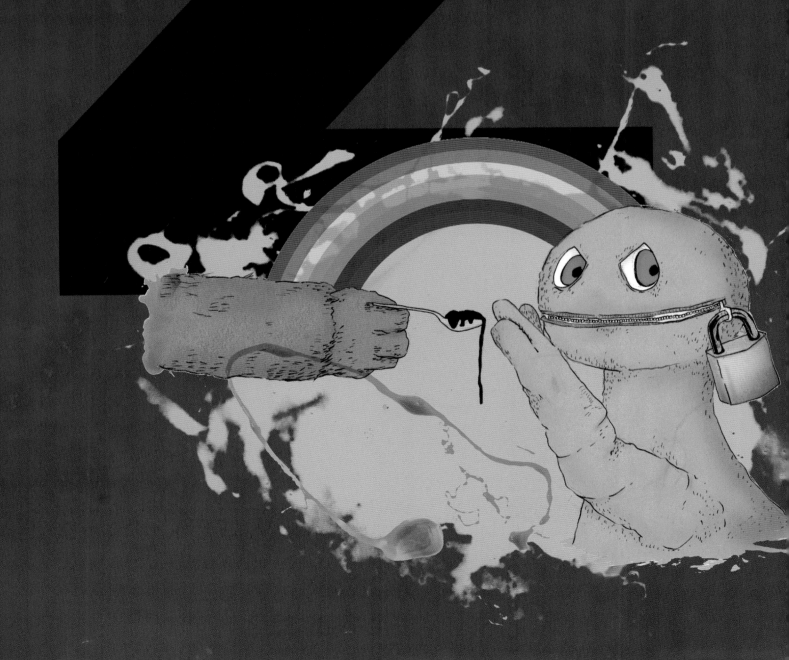

~OLD BURTON-ON-TRENT PROVERB~

C.1485

SOURCE UNKNOWN
(BUT LIKELY TO HAVE BEEN INEBRIATED AT TIME)

GOODBYES
THEY NEVER
DO COME EASY,
BUT RARER STILL
BE THEY YEASTY